A New Chapter

The Mick Whitburn Story

A New Chapter
The Mick Whitburn Story

Jill Gupta

First Published in 2000 by OM Publishing

06 05 04 03 02 01 00   7 6 5 4 3 2 1

OM Publishing is an imprint of Paternoster Publishing,
PO Box 300, Carlisle, Cumbria, CA3 0QS, UK
and Paternoster Publishing USA
Box 1047, Waynesboro, GA 30830-2047
www.paternoster-publishing.com

British Library Cataloguing in Publication Data

A catalogue record for this book is available
from the British Library

ISBN 1-85078-373-X

Cover design by Mephisto
Typeset by WestKey, Falmouth, Cornwall
Printed in Great Britain by
Cox & Wyman, Reading, Berkshire, RG1 8EX

Dedication

I would like to dedicate this book to my brother and sister in Christ, David and Angelique Tak, who have been a great source of encouragement and help to me since they have lived in England.

Thanks

Thank you to The Drummond Trust, 3 Pitt Terrace, Stirling, and Print and Promotions of Worthing for their financial assistance which made this publication possible.

Contents

One

Down and Out

'It was as well there was no violence used in this crime, or you'd be facing a long sentence. As it is, you will both go to prison for five years.' Five years for forty-five quid! I couldn't believe it. The judge must have been swayed by the pack of lies the police told in court. They said me and my mate Snake had worn masks and been armed with a shotgun. Our solicitor pointed out that there was no evidence to support these allegations, but it was too late. The impression of me and Snake as two vicious armed thugs, executing a cold-blooded, pre-planned crime, had had its influence on the judge and the truth of the matter would never come out in that courtroom.

The truth was that I had gone to the Pelican pub in Stroud that evening in October 1976 to have a few drinks with Snake. He'd only been out of prison for three or four days, having served a twelve-month sentence for robbing his old headmaster's house armed with an airgun. While he was inside, someone told him about a moneylender's place which was worth turning over. It seemed that the moneylender always kept around two grand in notes in an old biscuit tin and Snake was keen to get his hands on some ready cash. But he needed help and since I was up for anything, I agreed to meet him in the pub the following evening. If the coast was clear, we'd go for it. That night we borrowed a knife from Priest, one of the local bikers, and a car from a guy called Kevin Jenkins. I got in the car alongside Snake and he drove out of Stroud into the countryside.

It was about ten o'clock. The night was dry and clear. After five or six miles we turned off the main road into a narrow lane with high hedges on either side. Snake switched off the engine and the headlights and we coasted down the last few hundred yards, coming to a halt in front of a pair of cottages. One was unoccupied, the other belonged to the moneylender. The cottage was in darkness and there were no vehicles parked in the driveway or the lane. We checked the cottage front and back. Everything was quiet and still. The leaded panes of glass in the windows presented a problem, so Snake braced himself against the post of the porch and kicked the front door in.

I started to search the ground floor while Snake climbed the stairs. The sound of moaning made us freeze on the spot. It came from one of the bedrooms. I ran upstairs and joined Snake on the landing. We pushed open a bedroom door and the light from our torches shone straight into the face of a terrified woman. She was clutching the bedclothes to her throat and whimpering with fear. We told her we wouldn't hurt her and just wanted to know where the money was. At first she said there wasn't any money in the house, but when she realized we weren't going to leave until we found some, she told us the only money she had was in her handbag on a table downstairs.

I ran down to the hall, found the bag and sure enough there was a roll of fivers under a handkerchief. But the bag contained nothing else – no lipstick, purse or comb, so I knew from past experience that there would be more money hidden elsewhere. The cash in the handbag was there in case anyone broke in. They would find the money and, hopefully, be satisfied with that and leave. But we knew about the biscuit tin stuffed full of notes, so we looked for it everywhere, even under the mattress the woman was lying on! As time went on I became increasingly nervous. We'd found no sign of the tin and we'd already spent too long in the cottage. Snake was feeling as edgy as me, so we decided to give it up as a bad job and get away.

We were back at the pub before closing time. Snake gave Priest and Kevin a fiver each and we split the remainder between us. I spent my forty-five quid on hash and it took only two days for my share of the robbery to go up in smoke. It also took only two days for the police to catch up with me and Snake. As usual, I was in the Pelican enjoying a beer with Slimy, a biker brother of mine. Snake was playing darts with another bloke. Two plainclothes detectives walked in through the door and made straight for me and Snake. Despite Slimy's very vocal objections, they led us outside and searched us. I was carrying a small amount of marijuana, but they didn't find it. We were hustled into separate unmarked police cars and driven to Stroud police station. Despite being sandwiched between two officers, I managed to slide the sachet of dope down the back of the seat.

Snake and I were questioned separately, but I guessed he'd be doing the same as me – denying all knowledge of the robbery and insisting he was in the pub all evening. I stuck to the story, even after they showed me Kevin's statement, which declared that we had borrowed his car shortly before the robbery and returned it to him later that same night. The police didn't seem bothered by my unflagging insistence that I was not involved. They said they had enough evidence to charge us both, then they concluded the interviews and put us in a cell together, expecting us to see sense and plead guilty.

We sat on the thin plastic-covered mattress in the police cell and agreed that Kevin had dropped us in it. Snake reckoned that the woman in the cottage had somehow managed to get the car's registration number, which had led the police straight to Kevin. He had told them everything, including the fact that we paid him five pounds out of the proceeds of the robbery for the loan of the car. In the end we decided to plead guilty in the hope of receiving a lighter sentence.

After a night in the cells, we were taken to the magistrates' court where our legal aid solicitor appealed for bail. Bail was refused and we were remanded in custody for seven days. Later that day they took us to Gloucester prison. We appeared before the magistrates several more times during the following weeks. Bail was refused every time, but at last the case was referred to the crown court. Six months after the robbery had taken place, Snake and

I stood in the dock in Gloucester Crown Court and waited to hear our sentence. Since we had pleaded guilty there was no jury, just a panel of three judges who took on board the police lies about masks and a gun, and weren't too impressed that I had breached a two-year conditional discharge for shoplifting. Even then I was convinced that I'd be sent down for no more than three years and most likely only two. The five-year sentence left me speechless, but up in the public gallery Slimy voiced the first thought that came into my mind. 'Appeal against that, Mick, he don't know what he's on about.'

By the time we arrived back at Gloucester prison, the immediate shock had worn off and I was my usual jokey self. I tried to have a laugh with the prison officer in reception, but he just looked at me and told me that the realization of what a five-year stretch meant hadn't hit me yet. Still chuckling, I collected the cardboard box in which my civilian clothes would be stored. From now on I'd have to wear prison gear.

Two weeks later Snake and I were transferred to Bristol prison, where we were held while the authorities decided which prison we would serve our sentence in. It was a time of medical and psychiatric testing and an opportunity to lodge an appeal. It seemed certain that Snake and I would be split up, with me going to Albany on the Isle of Wight and Snake to Dartmoor, but Snake managed to sneak a look at the allocation list and discovered that we were both off to Dartmoor prison. After a month in Bristol, we boarded a coach and set off for one of the most notorious prisons in England.

Dartmoor prison is a bleak, dismal place set in a vast expanse of harsh moorland. A permanent grey mist seems to hang over the solid granite building, and a sense of heavy oppression settles on you as soon as you drive through the gates and under the inscription which, I was told, reads: 'Abandon hope all ye who enter here.' Inside, condensation runs down the cell walls and in the winter it is bitterly cold. The outlook was pretty bleak, but I still felt sure of myself and in control. After all, prison wasn't a new experience for me. I'd been there, done it and knew the ropes. That's how I got prison gear that actually fitted me and was fairly new. I carried the rest of the kit they'd given me to the wing and was shown into a cell.

It hit me two days later. I was sitting alone in my cell staring at a blank wall when I suddenly realized what being banged up for five years really meant. It was an unbearably long time. Tears of self-pity and frustration streamed down my face. I flung myself across the bed, buried my head in the pillow and sobbed. Although I knew that most prisoners cried at some time or another, that didn't help. Nobody would admit to giving way to tears, and I had to pull myself together and put on a hard front. Anger replaced the grief I'd felt and it spilled over when a prison officer told me to hurry up during slopping out. He got more than a mouthful back from me. The prison chaplain didn't fare much better. When he visited me I told him to get out of my cell. I wanted nothing to do with him or his church.

A week later I was sewing mailbags by hand! In every other prison the bags were stitched by machine, but not in Dartmoor. There were machines in the prison, but people like me were forced to do everything by hand to begin with. Just like prisoners of yesteryear, I sat on a hard wooden chair and waxed string by hand with black wax, then sewed two pieces of material together with a regulation eight stitches per inch. Get it wrong and you had to unpick your work and start again. Since we were paid piece rates it was important to get it right first time. It was mind-numbingly boring, with only the breaks to look forward to during the nine-to-five working day, but I worked hard, determined to earn a move into the machine shop where I could churn out loads of mailbags, and make quite good money to spend on tobacco in the canteen. It took five weeks, but my hard work paid off.

I was soon proficient at using my sewing machine and had time to chat to my fellow workers, without having to concentrate too much on what I was doing. Twister and Abbo were Hell's Angels from the Windsor chapter. With my biker background we soon became good mates. Twister supplied me with dope brought in by his visitors, while I supplied him with tobacco at the end of each week. We would roll joints in the exercise yard or back on the wing and even had the nerve to smoke them in the machine shop.

I became so involved with Twister, Abbo and another bloke, Fingers, who had his own outlaw group, Satan's Breed in Cardiff, that I grew further and further away from Snake and rarely thought of him. Six of us bikers formed a sort of club inside Dartmoor. We kept ourselves to ourselves, shunning the other prisoners whom we regarded as low life and avoiding the prison officers, who were the scum of the earth. The governor was rumoured to have been in charge of Parkhurst at the time of the riot there, but had not been sacked or disciplined, just moved to Dartmoor. One of the screws who'd robbed the petty cash in another jail had also escaped punishment and been relocated to Dartmoor. As far as we were concerned, whether you were a prisoner or a prison officer, if you were caught doing something wrong you ended up in Dartmoor, in the middle of nowhere.

Being so isolated made it all the more important to have mates who would stick with you through thick and thin. Our little group grew more tightknit than another jail had started a group called PMB (Prison Motorbike Brotherhood), we contacted them and subsequently set up our own PMB in Dartmoor. We tattooed PMB on our arms, grew our hair long and didn't shave. It meant declaring to the authorities that we'd become Sikhs, since they were the only inmates who didn't have to submit to the compulsory short back and sides. Twister had pulled this stunt during a previous stretch in prison and they'd made him wear a turban! In a year my hair grew so long the prison officers threatened to get a turban sent in for me, but it never happened.

After months of stitching mailbags, I was given a new job working in the blacksmith's shop. I had to drill holes in the metal cross strips that were made up into the bars for prison windows and gates. Over a year dragged by and I became due for my first parole reports. I tried not to get too excited, but I couldn't stop thinking that if I got my parole I could be out in six to nine months' time. What could go against me? I'd been put on report a couple of times – nothing serious, just a bit of backchat – but then there'd been the beard incident back when I was working in the mailbag shop. My beard had grown thick and bushy and, for a laugh, Twister plaited it into two forks like you get on the front of a motorbike. When I got back on the landing one of the screws told me to take the plaits out, but I refused. It was my beard and I'd do what I liked with it. A senior officer sent a direct order to me to unplait my beard, but I stood my ground. The next day I was up before the governor.

I stood to attention between two prison officers and gave my name and number. The governor listened solemnly to the evidence against me, then asked if I had anything to say or if I wanted to call a witness on my behalf. I didn't want to try and defend myself, I just wanted to hear my sentence and get on with it. It was in the governor's power to fine me and/or sentence me to solitary confinement for anything up to two months. If he wanted an offender held in solitary for longer than that, he had to call in a visiting magistrate who could sentence a man to solitary confinement until the time of his discharge. On this occasion I was fined three days' pay and released back on the wing. Needless to say, any hopes for parole were dashed. Life settled down again for a short while, then Twister and Abbo were moved to the carpentry shop.

Immediately I applied for a job change so that I could join them. The job was less taxing than the mailbag shop, so we took turns going into the toilet to smoke dope. Most days we were stoned out of our heads. Twister's Hell's Angels brothers from Windsor visited regularly and kept him well supplied with drugs, but I'd only had one visit in three years, so I had no way of getting drugs in from outside and had to rely on Twister, Abbo and the others to let me have some of theirs.

Then the prison authorities stepped in and gave me a massive helping hand. They arranged for me to go to Gloucester prison for accumulated visits. I'd spend about six weeks there and would be allowed as many visitors as I could persuade to come and see me! I knew I could rely on Slimy turning up every few days and smuggling in small amounts of dope each time. He'd been my sole visitor in Dartmoor, but had only come once because it was such a long and difficult journey. Since I'd been sent down he'd become a small-time dealer, selling in and around Gloucester and, thanks to the authorities, he was on hand to supply me with about quarter of an ounce of dope each visit. I had so much grass I was able to do trade-ins with other prisoners for pills. Then I got to share my cell with an Iranian and Monty, who was in the music business, and they introduced me to heroin. I had accumulated a large stock of dope to take back with me to Dartmoor, but the three of us smoked the lot in a matter of days.

Back in Dartmoor, and with only eighteen months of my sentence left to serve, I became eligible to apply for a job outside the prison. This meant more money, more freedom and the opportunity to smuggle in drugs for other prisoners. My hopes were high since my prison record was quite good. I'd managed to keep out of trouble despite hanging around with the Hell's Angels, because we all had the same aim – to get out of Dartmoor as quickly as possible. Cutting ourselves off from the other prisoners helped us to avoid bother and the danger of getting into debt, through borrowing tobacco, phonecards or anything else we wanted and couldn't wait for. My application was successful. I was given a job in the stables. I had to make up cow feed into solid pellets, tidy up the yard, feed the cows and drive the tractor. For most of the day I was on my own, so I had plenty of time to enjoy a joint behind the sheds.

The relaxed regime made it easy for me to make money from American tourists who came to take photographs. I would wear a prison issue blue and white striped shirt under another shirt, then strip off and sell the Americans the genuine HMP gear. During the months I worked in the stables I was never found out and after a while I asked for a move to the dairy, where there was more company, better food and a well-established routine for getting your hands on some extra cash, tobacco and weed.

Working in the dairy meant a six o'clock start and a twelve- to fourteen-hour day. We had a cooker in one of the stables, and were able to pick up food from the kitchens on our way out. We enjoyed freshly cooked breakfasts and baked cakes with ingredients that we managed to sneak out alongside the bacon, eggs, sausages and bread. The prison officer on duty in the farm office loved home-made cake, so he happily turned a blind eye to what was going on.

Every day I hitched up the tractor and drove out to the fields to feed the cows. A wall was all that separated me from the outside world. I never attempted to escape, knowing I was soon to be released, but I was more than willing to take a chance on collecting parcels thrown over the wall by prisoners' visitors and smuggling the contents to the inmates. Snake was working in the dairy too, so either he or I would pick up the parcel, take out our percentage and, over the next few days, slip the contraband past the screws and hand it over to its rightful owners. Since we came in and went out of the dairy frequently, we weren't strip searched, just frisked and our pockets checked.

Once a week we took a large laundry bag full of filthy overalls back into the prison with us. The laundry bag was a favourite way of getting packs of illegal substances through the gate. If they were found, no one individual could be blamed. The stuff would be confiscated and that was that. No one would lose his job or be put on report unless someone grassed him up or the screws were looking for an excuse to get at him. The bag went through unchecked except when there was a special security search at the gate, which rarely happened. Everything ran smoothly until a new inmate arrived at Dartmoor and was put to work in the dairy.

The day our successful smuggling scam was blown sky high started like any other. I went out to the fields on the tractor to feed the cows, then returned to the yard to find out if Snake had picked up the parcel. If not, I was going to do it. Before I'd had time to get down from the tractor, Snake was by my side. He looked shell-shocked and couldn't tell me the bad news fast enough. The new guy had found the parcel and given it to a screw. I thought Snake was winding me up, but when I realized he was serious my brain went into overdrive. Should I go and beat the guy up then and there, or wait until we were back in the prison where my other mates and the prisoner whose parcel it was could join in?

I was thinking it through when I saw the bloke walking towards the calves' shed. Lying on the ground near the entrance to the shed was an iron bar. It seemed to be an answer to my question. I leapt down from the tractor and ran after the man, pausing only to pick up the bar. I followed him into the shed and asked him, 'What's your game?' As he turned round to face me I hit him across the head with the iron bar. He fell into a crumpled heap, clutching his head. I tossed the bar into a corner of the shed and walked away. Within minutes another inmate who'd just heard about what had happened with the parcel went into the shed and gave the guy a good kicking.

Snake and I were the first to be pulled in for questioning by the security officers. Often the prison officers overlooked the presence of marijuana amongst the inmates to avoid stirring up trouble. They knew that trying to stop drugs coming in altogether meant constantly searching visitors and prisoners alike, which would result in rising tension and worsening relations between inmates and staff. Most of the time they used their own judgement about taking action or turning a blind eye, but they couldn't ignore the combination of a large parcel of dope and a badly injured prisoner. They suspected I was involved with bringing the parcel in and were sure that I had something to do with the guy being beaten up, but they had no proof, so they strip searched me, then pulled my cell apart. They were desperate to pin something on me.

After a lot of effort, they found some letters from Slimy which the censor had neglected to date stamp, and a guitar I'd brought back from woodworking class without permission. I was charged with smuggling letters into the prison and put on report. The governor sentenced me to fourteen days' solitary. When I came back on the block, I was sent to the mailbag shop. I was back where I'd started. Within a few weeks Twister, Abbo and Fingers joined me. It would have been like old times, but Twister and Abbo had only a couple of months to their discharge, so there was an atmosphere of suppressed excitement. They never stopped planning what they were going to do once they were released. One assignment was of paramount importance. They were going to take revenge on Slim Jim on Fingers's behalf.

Slim Jim was the leader of a bike club in Wales called the Renegades. While Fingers, who was president of a biker group known as Satan's Breed, was in prison, Slim Jim took advantage of his absence and tried to take the patches from his members. Twister and Abbo had an agreement with the Hell's Angels Windsor that they would back Satan's Breed, so as soon as they were out they took some of the Hell's Angels Windsor with them to Wales. They knocked on Slim Jim's door and, when his girlfriend opened it, they forced their way in. They beat up Slim Jim, then Abbo raped him and Twister raped his girlfriend. As they left, they warned Slim Jim that if he ever again attempted to take any members from Satan's Breed, the Renegades could expect trouble from Hell's Angels Windsor.

Six months later, Twister and Abbo were back in Dartmoor serving three-year sentences for assault and rape. During this time, I was refused a second parole report which meant that a few months on parole was the most I could hope for. Just to make things worse, the prison officers went on a work-to-rule. We knew this meant being banged up in our cells for twenty-three out of every twenty-four hours, but in fact we were allowed out of our cells for no more than fifteen minutes in every twenty-four hours and we received no mail during this time.

Frustration turned to anger, and every inmate protested by banging incessantly on the doors and the heating pipes. We made so much noise that it could be heard outside the prison walls. I knew the screws would pick on a few prisoners and accuse them of being the ring leaders, and that they were most likely to choose me and the other bikers. So I barricaded myself in and succeeded in getting the governor's attention. I told him about the mail, the lack of exercise and only being let out for quarter of an hour. The next day they started giving us exercise periods and brought our post to us, so I put my bed, locker and chair back where they belonged. The prison quietened down for a day or two, but being locked in a cell for such an interminable time was unbearable, and when a few inmates started banging again I joined in, even though I was sure it wouldn't achieve anything other than annoying the screws.

I didn't even hear them coming. Seven screws burst into my cell and told me to pick up my kit because I was going into solitary confinement. When I refused to move they grabbed me, kicked and punched me, then carried me struggling and shouting down the metal staircase. Still trying to fight back against insuperable odds, I screamed, 'Riot – they're giving me a kicking!' at the top of my voice. The next day I stood in front of the governor charged with inciting a riot. My body was bruised all over, I had two black eyes and I simmered with resentment because, although many other prisoners had been banging on their doors, the prison officers had targeted me and me only. This was what you got for being different, for being part of a small, tightly-knit group that kept itself to itself. Such behaviour marked you down as uncooperative, a threat to authority, someone who needed to be taught a lesson.

They marched me down to a strip cell and pushed me in, slamming the door behind me. I had a smock-type top, tracksuit bottoms, a plastic chamber pot and nothing else. No mattress, no blanket and no heating. It was bitterly cold. I wedged myself in a corner, wrapped my arms round my body, drew my knees up tight to my chest and tried to work out whether the governor would transfer me to another cell the following morning or leave me to freeze in this filthy stone box.

The next day I was informed of my sentence for attempting to cause a riot: twenty-eight days' loss of remission, twenty-eight days' loss of pay, twenty-eight days' solitary confinement. At least I was out of the strip cell! My new cell had a polished floor and a bed. The floor was concrete, which had been covered in boot blacking and polished to a high shine. The bed was made of boards with a thin mattress on top. It stood six inches off the floor. Some warders allowed you to keep the bed in the cell during the daytime, others made you prop it up outside the door so there was nothing to sit on.

I knew I could cope with solitary confinement – I'd done it before – but I wanted to get back at the people who'd picked on me. I was bitter and angry. As I thought about all the injustices I'd suffered, I wanted to explode. An order to clean the cell floor was the spark that set me off. I refused. They flung a mop at me just as you'd throw a spear at a wild animal. I didn't touch it. Exercise time came. I was allowed out of the cell for fifteen minutes. Just outside the cell door were two parallel white lines. I was supposed to walk between the lines when leaving or entering my cell. As I exited the cell I deliberately stepped on one of the white lines. It might seem childish, but it aggravated the screws and that was good enough for me. When I returned, my cell was inches deep in water. The mop had gone and in its place stood a bucket and a piece of cloth. I had no choice. I crouched down and started mopping up the water. After a while I realized it didn't matter that much to me – it helped to pass the time.

I was put back on the wing after I'd served my twenty-eight days. A few months later my final parole report came up. The most I could get was four months because of the trouble I'd been in during my incarceration. One of the panel members asked me what I intended to do once I was released from prison. 'Join the Hell's Angels and go round terrorizing old people,' I sneered at him. He didn't have a clue about me or the Hell's Angels. In fact, I had decided to join Fingers and the Satan's Breed. As soon as I was discharged, I made straight for Cardiff. When I arrived at the station, Sandy, the Sergeant at Arms for the club, picked me up on his Honda and took me to the clubhouse. They had a special treat arranged for my first night of freedom – a trip to Scotland. I found myself on a mission to take revenge on Paul Johnson, a guy who had ripped off the Windsor chapter in some motorcycle deals.

Two

Out and About

We started out for Scotland. I'd changed into a pair of old jeans with half a leg missing, courtesy of Sandy, and a jacket with Filthy Few patches on the back. The jacket belonged to a bloke called Black Rat who was in prison. He had been a member of the Filthy Few before he joined Satan's Breed. With my long, bushy hair, a beard down to my waist and tattooed hands and arms, I felt and looked like an outlaw biker even though I didn't own a bike! Sandy gave me a long, thin-bladed knife and Fingers handed me two acid tabs to take on the way back.

The driver, Stan, and his girlfriend sat in the front. Sandy and I took up the back seat with Fingers sprawled across us. We were anxious not to draw attention to ourselves, but it didn't help that Stan had only recently started to learn to drive. We thundered up the motorway just north of Bristol, half on and half off the hard shoulder. Stan was convinced that the hard shoulder was the slow lane. He refused to let Sandy take the wheel and we paid the price. A police patrol car flashed us to pull over and we screamed at Stan to brake slowly, to give us time to hide the knives and drugs down the side of the seats.

The police motioned Stan to get out of the car. As they questioned him, they kept staring suspiciously at the three of us in the back. Then they asked the girl to go over to the police car. Fingers, Sandy and I were going to tell the police that we were on our way to Stroud to see a mate, but Stan and his girlfriend hadn't decided in advance on their story, so they each told the police a different tale. The police radioed for another vehicle and we were all taken to the nearest police station for questioning.

My interrogation went something like this:

Name? Michael David Whitburn.

Date of birth? 22.1.55.

Where are you from? Dartmoor prison.

Very funny. What's your address? Dartmoor prison.

Don't play games with me. Where have you come from? I was discharged from Dartmoor prison this morning.

Then they searched me and found a driving licence in one of the jacket pockets.

What did you say your name was? Michael David Whitburn.

How come this driving licence says something else? That's because it's not my driving licence.

What's the name on the licence? I don't know.

What's it doing in your possession? It must have been in the pocket when I borrowed the jacket from Fingers' place.

Where does he live? Why don't you ask him – you've got him outside.

Where do you live? No fixed address.

Where did you sleep last night? Dartmoor prison.

Don't lie to me. You haven't come out of Dartmoor looking like that. Check it out if you like.

They put me in a cell while they checked it out. I was soon joined by Stan. Fingers and Sandy were put in the only other cell, which faced ours but was set at an angle to it. We had had to remove our boots and belts and, since it looked as though we were going to be there for the night, we asked for some blankets. While the police were questioning the girl, I amused myself by messing around with the cell door. I stretched my arm through the hatch used for passing food to prisoners and found I could reach the handle. To my surprise, the handle turned and the cell door opened. I walked through the doors at the end of the corridor, expecting to see the duty officer behind his desk, but there was no one to be seen. I could have walked free but, as we had done nothing wrong, I could see no point in making the police more suspicious of us by escaping. Instead I went to the room where I'd been questioned and opened the door. Two police officers swung round in unison and stared at me as if I were a ghost. 'Have you got the blankets yet?' I asked innocently.

'How did you get out? I thought I put you in a cell!' said one of them in amazement.

'You didn't lock the door,' I replied.The officer escorted me back to my cell and shut me in. As he walked back down the corridor, I put my arm through the hatch and tried the handle. I couldn't believe it when the handle turned under my hand and the cell door clicked open. I caught up with the policeman before he reached the end of the corridor. I tapped him on the shoulder. 'Don't forget the blankets, will you?' I said. Behind me I could hear Fingers and Sandy laughing like drains.

Grim-faced, the policeman took me back to the cell yet again. He checked the door several times before he was satisfied that it was firmly locked. He walked off, but I could see him peeping through the door at the end of the corridor every now and then, to make sure I hadn't got out.

After everyone had been interviewed and the addresses checked out, the police decided to charge Stan with driving without due care and attention and release the four of us without charge. We left on a high, knowing what a different scenario it would have been if they'd searched the car and found the knives and drugs. This helped to put in perspective the fact that my first night out after three and half years in prison had been spent doing a three-hour stretch in a police cell!

Stan and his girlfriend were told to get a train to Cardiff, while the rest of us got back into the car and, with Sandy at the wheel, made our way to Stroud to pick up Stompy. Stompy had been in Dartmoor at the same time as myself, Twister, Fingers and Abbo. We regarded him as an honourable member of Satan's Breed although he was not a patch holder. He was respected because he was always willing to help out whatever the circumstances. Stompy got in the car with Fingers, Sandy and myself and we set out once more for Fife with a list of the names of pubs where Paul Johnson might be found.

Sandy and Stompy took turns driving through the night and we arrived in Fife early the next morning. We had breakfast in a caff, then sent a postcard to Windsor to say that we had arrived in one piece and to prove that we were going ahead with our plan to sort Johnson out. We killed time until midday, then started checking some of the pubs on our list. It was difficult because we only had the pub names and no addresses. As we walked from pub to pub, we were confronted by six or seven members of an outlaw bike club from Fife. We could see trouble written all over their faces. One of them walked round us to see what patches we were wearing. Had they been members of the Blue Angels from Glasgow, it might have been curtains for us, but they weren't and, having seen our patches, they were all smiles and the heavily charged atmosphere lifted.

We explained what we were doing in Fife and they told us they knew where Paul Johnson did his drinking, but advised us to wait until later in the evening before we went to get him. Meanwhile they invited us back to their club house where we shared a few beers and joints. We spent a lot of time inspecting their bikes. A couple of bikes had hammer dents in the top of the petrol tanks and they had painted 'oouch' beside them. They explained that they had had a run-in with some skinheads and since then the skinheads tried to damage their bikes whenever they came across them parked up outside a pub.

At last it was time to go and find Paul Johnson. The club president sent two men with us to watch out for the police. They were going to wait at either end of the road and if the police came anywhere near while we were in the pub, they would drive past giving a long blast on their horns. We walked into the pub where Johnson was known to drink and gave it the hard men act. We were bikers and we had a reputation to live up to. I went from table to table asking the same question, 'Where's Paul Johnson tonight?' As each drinker denied even knowing Johnson, I'd give him a look of pure contempt, take a swig of his beer and move on. Then two men sitting at a table at the far end of the bar admitted that they knew Johnson but that we were out of luck – he was locked up in Barlinnie jail.

We went outside and motioned to our watch-outs. They drove over and we asked them if they could check whether Johnson was in prison or not. They promised they'd find out and we swapped calling cards and phone numbers. Having done all we could, we decided to head back for Wales.

On our way out of Fife we stopped at a chip shop for something to eat. It was in a quiet road, so I told Fingers to pull over while I got some cod and chips for the four of us. I had no intention of paying, but I meekly joined the queue and as soon as the man behind the counter had wrapped the fish and chips up, I grabbed them and ran out of the shop and up the road towards the car. Unfortunately the man behind me in the queue decided to play the hero and gave chase. He caught up with me and grabbed my denim jacket. I turned round and pushed him, but he wouldn't let go. The fish and chips landed in the gutter and, as we continued to struggle, Fingers reversed at speed towards us. He braked sharply and leapt out of the car, closely followed by Sandy and Stompy. The 'have-a-go hero' let go of me and fled back towards the chip shop. I brushed myself down, retrieved the fish and chips, and we headed out of Scotland tucking into a cold and greasy meal, which tasted great because I hadn't paid a penny for it.

I constantly committed minor offences like this. I was so used to being in and out of police stations and prisons, that even if I were caught and charged I knew I would only get a fine. Since I never paid any fines, in time I would end up back in prison serving a concurrent sentence for any outstanding fines, and the slate would be wiped clean.

Soon after we returned to Cardiff, the Windsor chapter confirmed that Paul Johnson was in Barlinnie prison. While he was there he was safe from us and I put my mind to being accepted as a full member of Satan's Breed. The normal length of time spent prospecting for a club is six months, and if you're not known to anyone in the club you have to hang around for a couple of months before you can prospect. Usually you can't wear a full set of patches until you become a member. Fingers allowed me to wear the Filthy Few patches on the jacket he lent me, proving how much he'd grown to like me while we were in Dartmoor together. This meant a lot to me, but I still felt an outsider because I hadn't got a bike. Then Bug Eye turned up. Bug Eye was a club member and he was on the run from the police. He arrived at the club house on a stolen bike and left it there as his ten per cent donation towards club funds. He wouldn't be without wheels for long. In the next couple of days he'd steal another bike and be off somewhere else, working on the principle that the more he moved around the less chance the police had of catching him.

The bike Bug Eye arrived on was a 650cc Yamaha. Normally a stolen bike would be stripped down and the parts sold for spares. Sometimes a bike would be chopped – made into a custom-built machine – but this was expensive and time consuming. Bug Eye had only made one change to the Yamaha – he'd replaced the number plates with false ones. Fingers told me I could have the Yamaha and do whatever I wanted with it, but Bug Eye warned me not to ride round on it for too long. With the bike and my prospect patches I felt part of the club for the first time. It was a great feeling, a mixture of power and solidarity. There was a sense of security which came from knowing that every member of the club was a brother who would always be there for you, ready to lie for you in court and stand beside you in a fight.

Within a few weeks of having the Yamaha I went on a run up to Stroud. I was pushing my luck riding a stolen bike with false plates, but in Stroud I met another biker I'd known from before my time in Dartmoor. He had a 500cc Triumph Daytona and was keen to swap it for the Yamaha. The Triumph was only just roadworthy, but it had a log book and even a couple of months MOT left on it. I made the swap and took the bike to Graham, a real wizard with machines. He wasn't a biker, but he knew the value of doing favours for club members. I found Graham busy doing a paint job on the tank of a chopped bike. He'd fashioned the tank to resemble a coffin and he was using an air brush to put on a design from *The Lord of the Rings.* Orcs, dwarfs and elves roamed against the background of a rocky hillside. Just looking at it, only part finished, sent a shiver down my spine. Over the next few days Graham stripped down the Triumph, sorted out the mechanical problems and gave it a respray. A few months later I was able to repay Graham by helping him steal some engineering equipment he needed from a warehouse in Stroud.

I spent a lot of time travelling between Cardiff and Stroud and it was just outside Stroud that my initiation took place. We met up at Stompy's house. Those who were already full members of Satan's Breed urinated and vomited over my jacket and jeans. I was not allowed to wash them and had to go on wearing the jeans until they fell apart. I put on a new pair underneath when the original pair was too tattered to wear by themselves. Soon after the initiation ceremony I had 'Satan's Breed' tattooed on my left arm. While we were in Dartmoor, Fingers thought he'd call the club Outlaws so I already had 'Outlaws Nomads m.c.' with a skull and cross pistons tattooed above my wrist, a coffin on the outside of my left leg and '666' on my left knee.

Now a full member of Satan's Breed, I moved into a squat in Blackwood in Wales with Fingers, Sandy and two club mummers. The front of the house looked out over some wasteland. There was a garage at the side where I kept my bike and an alley which ran along the back of the row of houses. We stored some of the weapons which had been at the club house in the squat – chains, a machete, an axe, knives and clubs. To this we added an old army revolver which Sandy had picked up on one of our frequent trips to Stroud. He didn't have any ammunition, but it would still come in useful. After all, if you stick a gun in someone's face they don't normally ask whether it's loaded or not!

One night when we got back from the pub Fingers went upstairs and, as he took a pee out of the window, he saw someone duck down in a ditch near the front of the house. He called out to me to ask if I could see anything. I hung out of the window and tried to focus on where he thought he'd seen the mystery figure and, sure enough, I saw a head pop up from the ditch then quickly disappear again. We moved away from the window and had a hasty and urgent discussion. It looked as though another club was planning an attack, so we ran downstairs to the front room and told everyone to grab a weapon. We'd no sooner armed ourselves with chains and clubs than the police were banging on the window.

Fingers shouted that we were claiming squatters' rights, but they said they were not there about the squat and demanded we open the door. We were convinced that they were lying and refused to let them in. Sandy had the gun on him. He was sweating because anyone who's served a five-year sentence is automatically banned from owning or handling a firearm for life. He gave the gun to one of the mummers and told her to hide it. There was a small upstairs window positioned right under the roof and she could easily slip the gun into the gutter. The other mummer went to make sure the back door was locked. The police ordered Fingers to open up. He tried to play for time to give the mummer a chance to get rid of the gun and the rest of us to dispose of the other weapons, but the police were getting impatient. They said they'd break the door down. Fingers still did his best to stall them.

There was a resounding crash as the police shoulder barged the door. Sandy flung himself behind it to try and delay the inevitable, but after a couple more attempts on the front door we heard the sound of wood splintering as the back door parted from its frame. Police officers with dogs ran towards us and Sandy, realizing it was all over, opened the front door just as an officer threw his whole weight against it. He came hurtling into the narrow hall. Sandy grabbed him, spun him round and sent him flying back out through the doorway. Then Sandy did something stupid. He reached under his jacket and pretended to pull out a gun. The police reacted instantaneously. Two officers drew their guns and pointed them straight at Sandy shouting, 'Armed police. Get down!'

Sandy flung open his jacket to show he wasn't armed and put his hands up. For a moment everyone seemed to freeze, and in that moment it struck me that this was no routine check on an empty house. The thought had scarcely registered before I was thrown to the floor alongside Sandy and Fingers. I lay there face down as my hands were cuffed behind my back. The two women were also handcuffed. They were taken away in separate police cars. We three were pushed into a van and handcuffed to the wooden bench seat which runs from the front of the van to the back. There we stayed while the police searched the house. We watched as they came out with the clubs, knives, the machete and the gun.

Back at the police station we insisted that the women had nothing to do with anything that had been found in the house – they were just spending the night with us. The women knew to say nothing and answered every question with 'no comment', so after two hours they were released. We followed their example, refusing to respond when the police claimed we were preparing for a gang war. Our usual plan – to let one brother take the blame, admit to the offence and say the others knew nothing about it – didn't work. Sandy was ready to take the charge, but the police wanted to get all three of us. The next morning we were charged jointly with being in possession of a firearm and other offensive weapons. I wasn't too surprised that the police hadn't believed my protestations that the wooden club was nothing other than a broken chair leg or that I'd never seen the gun before.

We stood in front of the magistrates in Blackwood and were swiftly remanded in custody. Our first visitor was Rags, the vice president of Satan's Breed. He came regularly, bringing in some puff and news of what was happening in the club. A week later we were back in the Blackwood magistrates' court. We knew we wouldn't get bail, so we stood proudly in the dock flaunting our colours. The magistrates looked at us as if we were mass murderers or the Kray twins plus one, so we turned our backs on them and said we refused to recognize the court.

The case was finally heard at Cardiff Crown Court. The judge was advised that the gun was old and ammunition was no longer available for it. Most of the other weapons charges were either thrown out or taken into consideration. We ended up with a nine-month prison sentence each, suspended for two years. So we walked free, but from then on we were constantly stopped and searched on sight by the police.

Contrary to what the police believed, we never went looking for trouble. When we went on a bike run it was for the ride and to have a bit of fun with a few drinks, drugs and women. Only if we had an audience would we act up to the reputation we undoubtedly had. Since the days when the Mods and Rockers ran riot in Brighton, the press has latched onto any trouble involving Hell's Angels or Outlaw bikers. Some American bike magazines perpetuate the image of bikers as violent criminals and the UK clubs try to live up to the American Angels. The tattoos and patches were an outward sign of how tough we were. Some of the patches could be worn only after you had earned them by committing acts of gross indecency in front of at least three full club members.

I didn't care what I did as long as it was in line with what was expected from a member of Satan's Breed. I used and abused anyone who wasn't a brother and never gave it a moment's thought. While I was living in Blackwood I had an affair with a woman solely in the hope of getting money out of her, and I nearly murdered a man.

The man was called Roger. He wasn't a biker but he knew Tracey, who was having an affair with

Fingers at the time. Tracey had a daughter who had just turned five. Roger borrowed a small amount from the child's birthday money, promising to pay it back in a couple of days. A week went by and the money was still owing, so I joined Fingers at Tracey's house and waited for Roger to turn up. Sandy was there too, and a guy who was prospecting for us known as Animal. Tracey and her little girl were out.

Roger knocked at the door and Animal opened it. As Roger came into the room Sandy told Animal to stand guard at the front door. Then he asked Roger for the money. Roger didn't have it. Sandy started to lose his temper. He shoved a poker into the open coal fire which blazed in the hearth and as it heated up he punched Roger in the back. Sandy was over six feet tall and well built. He kept punching Roger and asking him when he was going to pay back the money. Roger promised to get the cash in the next two days, but Sandy wasn't satisfied. He picked up a length of rope and twisted one end into a hangman's noose. All the time he was working on the rope he was screaming at Roger. Why hadn't he paid back the money? Why did it take so long to get such a small sum together? Roger made some sort of pathetic excuse which infuriated Sandy all the more. He grabbed Roger by the scruff of his neck, seized the poker, now glowing red hot, and held it millimetres from his right eye. 'Shall I burn your eye out or hang you?' he snarled. 'Let's hang him,' I said, picking up the noose and throwing it over the door. 'OK,' said Sandy, 'hanging it is then.' He thrust the poker back in the fire and started punching Roger around the room.

Roger was now so petrified that he wet himself. Sandy was disgusted and ordered us to take him to the bathroom. Animal and I went with Roger to make sure he didn't escape. He stood there shaking, unable to urinate. We dragged him back to Sandy swearing and cursing him all the way. We told Sandy he'd refused to go. 'That's it. Hang him,' said Sandy. I dragged Roger to the door and pulled the noose over his head, positioning the knot to one side of his neck just as I'd seen it done in cowboy films. I sat on an armchair and pulled the rope taut, trapping it under one leg. On the other side of the door Roger stretched up onto his toes to try and relieve the pressure on his throat, but I was gradually strangling him without even realizing it.

Sandy called a halt when he noticed that Roger was going a funny colour. He soon recovered once the noose was removed. We sent him away with the instruction to pay back the money that very day, and the threat that if he didn't come back we would come after him. Within two hours we heard a noise at the front door and there on the mat lay an envelope containing the money. Roger had posted it through the letterbox and run. Strangely enough, we never saw him again. For some reason he no longer wanted to go around with us!

About this time, Hell's Angels Windsor officially recognized us as an Outlaw club. Fingers suddenly began to get big ideas. He wanted to set up Hell's Angels Wales since there wasn't an Angels club in the country. Opinion was divided. Some thought it was a good idea, others were for it as long as Windsor approved and yet others felt we were too small a club to make such a transition. There were only fourteen full members and two prospects. Nevertheless, at our monthly meeting the motion was put to the vote. The joints had been passed round nonstop and there was plenty of wild talk about us controlling Wales. Everyone was stoned and when the moment came the majority voted for setting up Hell's Angels Wales.

Our most urgent need was for funds. We decided to take whatever we could wherever we could. One of our scams involved going round pubs and ripping people off through drug deals. Sandy, Fingers and I did dozens of pubs outside Cardiff. We'd go into the gents and ask if anyone wanted some acid. If we got a buyer, we'd sell him a piece of silver foil with nothing inside it. Sometimes an irate punter came back saying there was no acid in the foil. Instantly we'd surround him, make out he was trying to con us and tell him that he must have dropped the tab on the floor when he unwrapped the foil. No one argued with us when we started to get heavy. Before long we had the funds to get the patches made up to our specification by a local business.

It was while we were waiting for the new patches that we visited Tracey and all but demolished her house. Tracey had been expecting to move for ages. Her house was only meant to be temporary accommodation and she hated living there. She had already tried to speed up the moving process by setting fire to the place, but all she achieved was a visit from the fire brigade and a large black patch in her bedroom. Animal came round. He had just done a successful job and his pockets were stuffed with several hundreds of pounds in notes. We decided to party.

We bought the local mini mart's entire stock of McEwans Export and got stuck in. Part way through the evening, Fingers found the machete and suggested that if we hacked all the doors off, the council would have to rehouse Tracey straight away. Fingers made a start and the rest of us tried to find other ways of hastening Tracey's move. It turned into a bizarre game. Destroy some part of the house, drink a can of beer, balance the empty can on a pile that was being built across the fire place and up towards the ceiling, then keep repeating the sequence until you passed out.

I woke up the next morning surrounded by splintered wood, broken glass and empty beer cans. We were kicking the cans around the back garden when the police arrived with some council officials and workmen. The workmen boarded up the house, then the police escorted Fingers and me out of Blackwood. They warned us never to return – or there'd be real trouble.

Back in Cardiff we started wearing our Hell's Angels Wales patches. Almost immediately we received threats from Hell's Angels Windsor and Hell's Angels England. At this time Windsor was at war with England, so we knew that if we carried on wearing Hell's Angels Wales we would be on our own. The subject came up at our next meeting, but it wasn't a matter for discussion. Fingers made a statement: we had to keep Hell's Angels Wales, otherwise we would lose the respect of other bikers and clubs.

Despite Fingers's brave words, the club started to fall apart under the pressure. On one occasion we went to Cannock to visit Fingers's brother, hoping to persuade him to move to Wales and join us. We were at a club that he frequented when we were told that Hell's Angels Wolverhampton were on their way to get us. They were tooled up and looking for action. We made a quick exit. There was no way that we few could hold our own against such odds. We hid our bikes in a friend's garage and went back to Fingers's brother's flat, where we began to make petrol bombs in case the enemy found out where we were holed up. The flat was on the second floor and we reckoned that we would be able to hold off any attackers and maybe even force them to give up. Luck was with us that night, and we stayed in the flat until early the next morning without a sign of any trouble. We collected our bikes and rode back to Wales.

Soon after this some members of the club decided to leave. They were good solid brothers and we'd only been flying the angel patches for a short while. There hadn't even been time for me to have them tattooed on my arm. I was gutted, but worse was to come. Sandy, the one I really respected and spent most of my time with, handed in his patches. It made me think that perhaps I should do the same. I talked it over with my girlfriend, Susan. She was keen to leave Cardiff and go back to Stroud where her parents lived, so the next day I quit the club. According to the rules, I should have left my bike as a donation to the club, but I decided to take the Triumph with me as I reckoned the club wasn't going to exist for much longer. Susan and I packed up and set off for Stroud.

The first few months were a struggle. We were dossing down on Ian's floor and finding it difficult to get enough money together to keep going. I spent most nights cruising around the lanes with Ian trying to find places we could break into. When we got really desperate, Susan would sneak over to her parents' house while they were both out at work and help herself from her mother's purse. I would wait for her at the end of the road. One day she came running down the road in a fine old state. I thought she'd been caught out so I revved up the engine and shouted to her to jump on quickly, but when she got to the bike she told me to wait – her mother was in and wanted to meet me!

Susan's parents lived in a nice house. When we first started going out Susan told them I was a biker and they were horrified, so we'd never met. In fact they did their best to keep us apart, even forcing Susan to choose between them and me. She chose to leave home and move in with me in Wales.

I wheeled the bike up to the house, wondering what sort of reception I was going to face. Susan's father wasn't there and I did my best to charm her mother. We talked and I got the impression that she quite liked me, even though I was dirty and scruffy. When she asked where we were staying Susan chipped in with 'in a van', before I could answer. Since this was the story Susan had obviously spun to her mother, I backed her up. After I finished my cup of tea, I carried it out to the kitchen. This simple action, and our long chat with not a single swearword uttered by yours truly, swung it for me. Susan's mum liked me and the atmosphere between us was so friendly that I let her take a pair of scissors and trim my beard and hair.

A few days later Susan's parents got in touch to say that they were searching for a place where we could stay. In less than a month they found us a flat just outside Stroud. Susan's mum spoke to the landlord and told him I had a bike which I needed for work. She didn't tell him that my job was chief beer taster at a local bikers' pub! They paid the deposit and we moved in. It was great having somewhere of our own. We managed to get hold of some furniture and Ian and I broke into a shop, loading up his car with enough shopping to last us a month. When Susan pushed me to do some decorating I quite happily picked up a brush and painted the living room. I felt that everything in my life was getting sorted and that the future was rosy. Then, one night at the pub, Fingers turned up with eight or nine bikers whom I'd never seen before. I knew they wanted my bike and that there was nothing I could do to stop them.

Fingers didn't beat around the bush. He told me he'd got the club back together and I'd be welcome to rejoin it, but if I declined his kind offer they would take the Triumph. I thought I was going to get beaten up and lose the bike, but Fingers was willing to talk – and listen. I explained that I couldn't go back to Wales and that I really wanted to keep the bike. As I hadn't any money to give them, could I buy the bike over a period of time or do the club a favour in return for them letting me keep it? Usually a favour involved doing over someone who had ripped off or badmouthed the club. Despite my best efforts at persuasion, Fingers wasn't interested in any deals. He loved Triumphs and he was determined to take either me and the bike back to Cardiff or just the bike.

When he said he wouldn't mind staying in Stroud overnight, I invited him and his mates to crash out at my flat. I was hoping it would give me a chance to talk him round.

There wasn't an inch of empty floor space in the living room with eleven blokes squashed in together. The music was thumping out, the joints were being passed around and I was deep in conversation with Fingers, so I didn't notice Susan slip out. I talked to Fingers until one in the morning, but to no avail. The others crashed out, having amused themselves by drawing all over my freshly painted walls. The next day, when they were ready to leave, Fingers started the Triumph and pulled out on to the road. As he opened up the throttle the engine coughed, spluttered and died. Fingers rolled to a halt.

We spent ages pushing the bike up and down the road, trying to bump start it, but after countless attempts we gave up. Fingers asked if I'd had any trouble with the Triumph before and I said no. I was as puzzled as the rest of them. Fingers decided to set off for home and to return at a later date to collect the bike. As they started up their bikes, an infuriated landlord came storming out of the block of flats, and made it plain that he would never have rented the flat to me if he'd known I was a biker. This did not go down well with the Cardiff contingent and they showered him in dust and gravel as they drove away at speed.

I pushed the Triumph off the road, still wondering what on earth was wrong with it. Susan soon put me out of my misery. It was down to her. She had poured water into the fuel tank to prevent Fingers from taking it! I spent the next five minutes rolling around the floor in fits of hysterical laughter. Then I drained the petrol tank, removed the carburettor, dried it with Susan's hairdryer, put in some unadulterated petrol, replaced the carb and the bike was as good as ever. Since this was the limit of my mechanical knowledge, it was just as well she did nothing more serious to the Triumph.

I had my bike, but I didn't have a club. Susan had immersed herself in making improvements to the flat, but I couldn't get that interested. So when I was invited to a party at the club house of an outlaw group called the Wolves, I jumped at it. Slug, whom I'd known before I did my five stretch, was a member and he introduced me to the club president, Legion. The club house was in Cheltenham and I was very impressed. It was a three-storey house standing across the road from a cricket field. The Wolves had had a lot of hassle from the neighbours who were doing all they could to get them evicted, but they had bought the house and were paying the mortgage.

The party was something else. Joints were provided free, the beer was fifty pence a can and if you began to get tired, someone would come round with a long line of speed for a pound. A favourite party trick was having a blowback against the wall. You had to be out of your head to agree to participate. You squatted down and stood up several times to empty your lungs and squatted down for the last time, expelling any remaining breath. Then a brother would put the lighted end of a joint in his mouth and you would draw on the other end. As you slowly stood up, inhaling all the smoke, he'd be blowing on his end to make it burn faster. Then as soon as you had breathed out all the smoke, the others would form a circle and spin you from one to another, then suddenly let you go so that you spun off, hit the wall and collapsed in a heap. When you started to show signs of life you'd get a free line of speed to get you back into the party spirit again. This particular party went on for two days nonstop.

When I'd got my head back together I asked Legion if I could prospect for the Wolves. One of the rules was that you had to live in the club house while you were prospecting. I went home and told Susan what I planned to do, and asked her to stay with me in the club house. It meant giving up the flat and Susan had other ideas. She wanted a nice home of our own with no involvement with bikers, other than the occasional fun night out. A row developed and I packed my bags and left her in tears.

Driving down the road with bin bags full of my clobber tied on with bits of string was not easy. The bike was wobbling all over the place and my head was still pretty wobbly after that party! I decided to turn round and head for Ian's place where I could dump my stuff until someone could bring it over to Cheltenham by car. Ian said I could leave my belongings with him as long as I wanted, so I set off again. I was heading down the road through Stroud when I realized that something didn't feel right. The wind was blowing through my hair! I'd left my skid lid at the flat.

As luck would have it, a police motorcyclist stopped me on my way back. I spent hours at the police station while they checked out my story, but I was finally released after being charged with driving without a crash helmet, having no insurance and riding a 500cc bike with a provisional driving licence. When I made it back to the flat to pick up my helmet, Susan tried to persuade me to change my mind about joining the Wolves, but I gave her a straight choice – to come with me or stay on her own at the flat. She burst into tears and I walked away, never to see her again.

I was given a room in the club house with just a mattress on the floor. I had to share the space with a bike which had been stripped down and resprayed, and I was warned not to scratch any of the parts. It was difficult to get my money from Social Security transferred from Stroud to Cheltenham and Legion reminded me after the first week that my rent was due. During those first few days in Cheltenham the police had stopped and searched me on three separate occasions. They didn't charge me but made it clear that they were watching me. This meant I daren't try any breaking or entering and I certainly didn't want to get a job, although a number of the bikers did work. But I needed more than the Social Security would pay and I couldn't see a way to get any extra cash.

For once I had to think seriously about what I was going to do. I toyed with the idea of going back to Susan or leaving the area altogether. But where could I go and what would I do? For some reason I started thinking about Basingstoke. Maybe I could contact some old school friends or even see if my parents still lived there. I made up my mind. The next morning I went to the Social Security offices as soon as they were open and asked for the money to buy a one-way ticket to Basingstoke. I left the Triumph with the keys in the ignition at the club house and walked away without a word to a soul.

Three

Past Times

I put the carrier bag containing the few possessions I'd brought with me on the floor between my legs, and settled myself into a window seat. It was getting dark and there was nothing much of interest to see as the coach rolled steadily towards Hampshire, so I closed my eyes and let my thoughts drift.

I pictured the first home I ever knew, 10 Casino Avenue, somewhere between Camberwell Green and Herne Hill in south London. I was born in Gipsy Hill, but my memory didn't stretch back to the time I lived there. But Casino Avenue I could remember – home to Mum and Dad, my elder sister, Helen, and brother Timothy and me, Michael. My baby brother, James, was born while we were living at that address. My grandparents lived nearby in Camberwell Green, only a short bus ride away. We visited them regularly.

I smiled to myself as I saw in my mind's eye the little boy who was me, playing in the small park at the bottom of the avenue. My favourite pastime was to balance a piece of wood on a roller skate, sit astride it and race down the hill. I loved a bit of excitement and danger even then!

The coach pulled up sharply at red lights, jerking me forward in my seat. It reminded me of the occasion when a coach didn't stop in time and I ended up in hospital. It must have been when I was about seven years old. The memory of what happened, when I ran across Red Post Hill straight into the path of an oncoming vehicle, is as fresh as if it happened yesterday. The impact threw me up the road and I lay there confused, dazed and hurting. It was my fault. I was late for school and Timothy had gone on without me. I was racing to catch him up and ran out into the road without looking. My jaw was broken, but otherwise my injuries were only minor, so I was soon back at Bessemer Grange Primary.

On Sundays, my two brothers and I were sent to Sunday School at the Methodist church at the top of Red Post Hill. My parents weren't church-goers but Sunday School was a convenient place to send us while they cleared up the house and prepared dinner. My sister had to stay at home and help Mum and Dad.

My family was working class. Dad was a welder. He worked for the Morris Singer foundry making bronze statues, such as the animal figures you can still see in Crystal Palace Park. Mum worked there in the kiosk part-time, to help make ends meet. Once a year we would go on holiday and, whenever we could, we'd go for days out. Dad had a motorcycle and sidecar. He would drive with Mum sitting pillion and we four children sat in a row in the sidecar! The best seat was the one at the front, because there was a small window in the nose of the sidecar and you could see through it if you wriggled down. Twice a year we visited a family who lived in Shoreham-by-Sea. The journey involved a very steep hill and the bike would struggle to get to the top. Although it always made it, the tension and excitement in the sidecar never failed to make this particular trip great fun.

On weekdays we three boys would listen out for the motorbike and race outside when we heard Dad pull up. We all wanted to have a go at riding pillion. Dad would take us round the avenue one at a time, then come indoors and settle down with the paper and his roll-ups, while Mum prepared the evening meal and we kids played. One day Dad came home on foot. The bike had broken down and when a friend offered to give him a lift to work in his car every day, Dad decided to leave the bike at home. On the first day of this new arrangement, Dad came back to discover that someone had broken into the sidecar and stolen his tools. After this, nearly every day something would be stolen from the bike or sidecar, so Dad got rid of it and started to learn how to drive. Once he'd passed his test, he bought a Morris Oxford. We were going up in the world!

My days at primary school ended and I started at the same secondary school Timothy attended. He went with his friends and I travelled to school with my best mate, Tommy White. The journey involved a short bus ride to Herne Hill, then two stops on the train. Once the novelty of going to a new school had worn off, we spent our time messing around. We took the light bulbs out of the carriage and threw them at passing trains. Sometimes we'd lift out the bottom part of the seat and sling it out of the window, in an attempt to get it to lie across the tracks. This feat was never achieved as the seats bounced as soon as they hit the ground. The bus offered a different challenge. It became a matter of principle only to board and get off a bus that was moving. One day Tommy jumped off and was running along in the same direction as the bus, so he wouldn't fall, when he ran straight into the bus stop and broke his arm! Despite being in a plaster cast he still had to jump on and off a moving bus, and he gave me plenty of laughs as he struggled to cope with his extra handicap.

Like most kids, we preferred to spend our dinner money on chips, although it was against school rules. An illicit visit to the chip shop resulted in a second road accident for me. Tommy and I saw some prefects coming to check on who was in the shop, so we ran back towards school. I was racing along like the wind and so intent on what I was doing that I didn't stop to think. I shot out into the road from behind a parked ice cream van and was hit by a car. My leg was bruised from the knee to the hip. Someone put a coat over me as I lay on the pavement and a crowd began to gather. Timothy joined the crowd out of curiosity, but when he saw the victim was me, he was horrified. He stayed with me and travelled alongside me in the ambulance to King's College Hospital. Mum arrived within the hour, but the damage was limited to severe bruising, so I was able to go home and enjoy being the centre of attention for a while.

There was soon even greater excitement in the family which overshadowed my brush with death. Dad's firm was moving out of London to Basingstoke. We would be moving there too, and had been allocated a brand-new council house. Before the big move Dad drove us down to Basingstoke to see our new home. It was on the Oakridge Estate and was one of the few already completed. The rest of the estate was one big building site strewn with JCBs, cement mixers and dumper trucks. At the bottom of the road we could see massive earth-moving machinery flattening out a chalk mound, so the construction firm could start building a ring road. Beyond that the countryside stretched out to the horizon, although in a short time the fields would disappear under another huge housing estate.

We moved during the summer holidays in 1969. In September Timothy and I started at the Charles Chute Secondary Modern. Just as in London, we soon formed our own separate circle of friends, but while Timothy settled down to his studies, I had virtually no interest in school work at all. I was into messing around. If there was nothing better to do after school, my friends and I would ride around the building site on the dumper trucks. Most of them had starting handles so you didn't need an ignition key to start the engines. We'd have races all over the site and it was a wonder that none of us got hurt. Sometimes we'd go to Sherbourne St John, a small village two miles from Basingstoke. One day we were trespassing on someone's farm, playing about on a tractor. We took a fag break, propping ourselves up against a haystack. Then one of my mates chucked a lighted match into the haystack and it went up in flames. Even we were taken aback by the enormity of what he'd done, and we legged it across the field and escaped into a wood.

In school I sat at the back of the classroom with two or three friends. I was totally oblivious to everything else that was going on. The first time I got the cane in my new school was because I went on carving my name into the desk lid, not realizing the headmaster was standing over me. The next occasion was on a cold winter's day. The teacher hadn't arrived and the classroom was chilly, so I decided to light a small fire in my desk to warm my hands. I opened my desk, tore some pages from an exercise book and crumpled them up in one corner. I pushed my textbooks to the other side of the desk, then set light to the paper and held my hands out to the warmth of the flames. The teacher entered the room. I quickly shut the lid of the desk and sat there with an innocent look on my face. Smoke began to curl out through the cracks in the lid so I leant forward and attempted to cover the cracks with my arms. The smoke found another outlet – the ink well. I cupped my right hand over it, but by now the teacher was suspicious. He came over to me and told me to open my desk. As soon as I lifted the lid, a cloud of smoke billowed out and flames shot upwards. In the confined space my books and the bottom of my wooden desk had caught fire. The teacher ran to get a bucket of sand and successfully extinguished the blaze. I got six of the best, the headmaster choosing the thinnest out of his collection of canes to cause me the greatest possible pain.

My best friends were Albert, Martin and Georgy. Like me they enjoyed mucking about, and we spent all our breaks and dinner times together. We would often go to a local sweet shop and steal sweets. If we had any money, we would buy a packet of five Park Drive cigarettes or Woodbines and smoke them on our way back to school. Most of the stolen sweets were wasted because we'd throw them around the classroom, creating chaos just before a lesson.

The school ran a youth club designed to keep people like Albert, Martin, Georgy and myself off the streets and out of trouble. Instead it gave us fresh opportunities to get up to no good. The members of the youth club took it in turns to do the disc jockeying. The record player was set up in the office and two youngsters would be allowed to go into it and choose which records were to be played that evening. One particular night Georgy and I were told we could be the disc jockeys.

While we were in the office, we looked in all the cabinets and desk drawers to see what we could find. One of the drawers contained twelve collecting tins. From the weight of them it was obvious there was quite a lot of money waiting to be counted and passed on to a national charity. We took six of the heaviest tins and dropped them out of the window on to the grass below. After the session had ended we picked them up and set off for home, stopping on the way at a piece of wasteland. There, out of view of any nosy parkers, we smashed the tins open with bricks and stones. We divided up the cash between us. I hid my money under the mattress and enjoyed working out how I'd spend my ill-gotten gains.

The next day Georgy and I boasted of how clever we'd been to leave six of the tins in the drawer. We reckoned nobody would notice that half a dozen had disappeared, but when the teacher who ran the youth club pulled us out of our lesson, we realized we hadn't been smart enough. He took us to an empty classroom and told us why he knew we must be the culprits. We were given an ultimatum – we could own up and return the money or he would call in the police.

We admitted our guilt and told him that the money was, as yet, unspent. The teacher said he would call at our homes that evening to collect the cash and tell our parents what had happened. My parents were furious with me and from then on my father questioned me whenever I said I was going out. He couldn't trust me any more.

Four

Back Home

The coach shuddered to a halt. I stretched and rubbed my eyes, dragging my thoughts away from the past. That was then and this was now. I made my way to the town centre, where I caught a bus to Oakridge Road. I noticed a lot of changes on the way, but the place was still recognizable. But were my parents still living in Mullins Close? If they'd moved I'd have to try some of my old mates, but, if the worst came to the worst, I'd find an empty house to break into. That would do me for the night.

I got down at Oakridge Road and walked the short distance to Mullins Close. The woman who answered the door was a stranger, a stranger who knew nothing of my parents. I tramped back through the estate towards the school that I used to attend. As the school came into view, I thought of all the people I'd left behind and hadn't contacted in over ten years – my parents, uncles, aunts, cousins. I decided to try my Uncle Colin. He lived in a different part of the estate with his wife Martina and three kids, Linda, Hilary and Scott. Colin and Dad had never got on too well, so when I was young I rarely saw him and his family, but if they were still in Millard Close, they'd certainly know Mum and Dad's new address.

Linda answered the door. She and Martina were alone in the house and they were amazed to see me. They brought me up-to-date with all the family news, and explained that Mum and Dad were living in a bungalow in Old Basing, two miles out of Basingstoke. Linda offered to drive me there, but said she'd drop me outside the door. Relations between Dad and Colin had worsened over the years. Linda didn't hang around. She pulled up outside the bungalow and, as soon as I was out of the car, she drove away as fast as her ancient Ford Cortina would go.

I walked up the short drive. Dad was busy washing the Volvo. He didn't hear me approach. His hearing had been impaired for years and he had to wear a hearing aid. I stood just behind him and said, 'Hello.' Dad turned round, took one look at me and said, 'Whatever it is you're selling, I don't want any.'

'You don't recognize me, do you?' I asked. It wasn't surprising – my beard was long and straggly, my hair stuck out like a tangled bush and my clothes were stiff with dirt and grease. Dad looked at me properly. His mouth dropped open in astonishment and disbelief as he realized who I was, then he wrapped his arms around me and gave me a big hug. He took me by the arm and led me to the kitchen door at the back of the bungalow. When he tapped on the window Mum peered out. 'Look who's here!' he shouted. For a few seconds Mum stared at me uncomprehendingly. Then she silently mouthed one word: 'Michael.'

After my parents had recovered from the shock I'd given them, they wanted to know what I'd been doing for the last ten years. I started haltingly, explaining that much of the time had been spent in prison, but as I talked I found I was able to open up and I told them everything. Dad was shocked at some of things I'd done, but heartened by the knowledge that I was telling the truth and not trying to make excuses for my behaviour. I said I'd come back to Basingstoke to get away from the Hell's Angels and to sort my life out, then I waited for their reaction. They were good, law-abiding people and had every reason to ask me to leave. But deep down I was desperate for them to accept me for what I was. There was no dramatic decision, no emotional outburst. Mum just asked if I was hungry and went to the kitchen to make me tea.

Meanwhile Dad offered me the spare room for as long as I needed it.

I was shaken by their response. It seemed so natural and low key and yet what they were doing showed how much they cared for me, even though I'd scarcely given them a thought for a whole decade. I talked to them all evening. They told me that my younger brother, James, still lived at home. He was the manager of a local pub and rarely got back before midnight. After hours of talking my parents decided to go to bed. I asked Dad what would surprise James most – coming home from work and finding me sitting in the front room or getting up in the morning to discover me eating breakfast in the kitchen?

I chose to stay up and caught James's eye as he crunched up the gravel drive and stared into the lighted room where I was watching television. By the time he entered the front room he'd sussed who the stranger in the armchair was and he was really pleased to see me. He produced a bottle of brandy that he'd been saving for a special occasion, and insisted on opening it to celebrate my return. We sat up most of the night talking and drinking.

Over the next few days I made myself presentable and caught up with other members of the family. My sister didn't have much trouble recognizing me because I'd had my hair cut, my beard shaved off and wore a new outfit which Dad had bought for me. When I last saw her, Helen was married with one little girl, Teresa. It was Teresa who answered the door when I called on the off chance at my sister's house. She didn't remember her uncle Michael, and I wouldn't have known who this bright young girl was if I'd met her outside her own home, she was so grown up.

Helen was thrilled to see me and introduced me to the new additions to her family – another girl, Fiona, and a boy, Robin. Life had been good to them. Helen's husband had worked his way up to the position of foreman. He had a new company car every two years, and they'd bought their own house, just behind the school I had gone to. I was pleased. I liked my brother-in-law. When he was dating my sister, he was into motorbikes and took me for rides on his 200cc Triumph Tiger Cub. Now, so many years later, he was still friendly and generous. Most impressive of all was his genuine offer of somewhere to stay, if things didn't work out for me at my parents' place. With three kids they didn't have a spare room, but were happy to take me in regardless. It meant a lot to me to have a bolt hole if I ever needed it.

Of my immediate family, only Timothy remained. He was a sergeant in the police force, living in London, and he kept in close contact with the family. When we met, a week or so after my arrival in Basingstoke, he offered me all the help in the world – as long as I really meant to change my ways. Timothy gave me one of his suits and I got myself a job at a building site. I was working as a hod carrier and earning good money. In my spare time I often helped my brother-in-law out doing private work.

By now I had settled down well, both to work and to living with my parents. One day, out of the blue, the police came to the bungalow looking for me. I'd committed several offences in the recent past and thought I'd got away with them. Was that why they had come? Or had the Hell's Angels, realizing I'd gone for good, given them my name to get themselves off the hook for some misdemeanour? Dad gave me a quizzical look, but left me alone with the officers in the dining room.

Being on my best behaviour, I invited them to sit down and asked how I could help them. They asked if I had been living in Stroud. When I admitted that I had, my voice was so shaky that they rushed to reassure me. I had nothing to worry about, they promised, they just needed to eliminate me from their inquiries. Did I know a man named Tim Burnham? I said he was an acquaintance, but I didn't know him well because, although we often went to the same pubs, he was not a biker like me and my mates.

Then they dropped the bombshell. Tim Burnham had been murdered. His body had been found in a plastic sack at the bottom of a lake. The blood drained from my face. I felt faint. A lot of thoughts had raced through my head when I'd seen the police at the door, but I never imagined they'd be questioning me about a murder. Again the police tried to put my mind at rest, assuring me that they only wanted to eliminate me from the list of suspects. Nevertheless they made careful note of the date when I left Stroud and got my parents to confirm that I had been living in Basingstoke with them since that time. They went, apparently satisfied with the information they'd gleaned from us, but for weeks I felt sick every time I relived the experience of being interviewed by the police in my parents' home.

The months flew by, and I started going out more frequently with my mates from my schooldays. They were all into drugs in a small way, smoking dope and using speed, mainly at weekends. I spent most of my free time with them. We had a laugh, talking about the old days, and they took me to pubs and clubs that were new to me. I made friends with people from work too and, by and large, I enjoyed myself. I wanted to do things right and live a straight life, but there seemed no harm in snorting a couple of lines of speed when I went out. In fact I convinced myself that speed kept me out of trouble. It stopped me getting drunk and, by the time it wore off and the alcohol started to take effect, it was time to go to bed and sleep it off, ready for work in the morning. Since I was earning good money I was never tempted to steal or sell drugs. I did miss having a bike and when

I finally decided to buy a little 125cc Yamaha and take a driving test, I proved to myself how serious I was about going straight.

Despite all my good intentions, I still couldn't stop myself from pretending the Yamaha was really a big bike and sometimes I rode it that way. One evening, driving along the country lanes between Old Basing and Basingstoke, I recklessly cut off a corner but didn't have the power to avoid a car coming in the opposite direction. No one was hurt, but the front of the bike was twisted. My old school friend Albert offered to sort it out. He was a good mechanic and could have made a decent living from it, but he would start a job, then lose interest and end up bodging it to get it finished. I said, 'Thanks, but no thanks.' This was the new me, riding a bike that was legal, above board and fully insured! I took and passed my motorcycle test and, to celebrate, I bought a Datsun and put in for my driving test. I passed first time after only a couple of lessons.

I had somewhere comfortable to live, a good job, money, wheels, a girlfriend, family, friends and a great social life. What was I missing? The buzz that comes from injecting speed into a vein, according to the people I was now spending most of my leisure time with. Albert and Georgy from school introduced me to a friend of theirs, John Greenbank. John was a small-time dealer and he gave us good deals. He lived with his common-law wife, Lyn, and stepdaughter, Hazel. We'd go round to his house at least twice a week. John, Albert and Lyn kept trying to persuade me to inject, but I resisted. I said I didn't want to become a junkie or to catch AIDS from using someone else's syringe.

Then, one day, we went to London, to Piccadilly Circus to score some speed. Albert, Lyn and I waited in the car while John went out to get the gear. He came back saying he hadn't been able to buy any speed, so he'd got some amps instead. This is a prescription only drug. It can be used as a heroin substitute and comes in liquid form in a small glass capsule. It can be taken only by injecting into a vein. John had four amps – one each. I'd held out for ages against injecting drugs: now in the back of John's car, I not only allowed Lyn to inject me, but I insisted on having the full contents of the amp shot into my bloodstream, and not just half as Lyn recommended. I couldn't move. I fell into a light sleep then woke up suddenly, only to doze off again and then wake. The cycle repeated itself again and again. Albert was driving and I remember wondering how he could drive under the influence of this mind-numbing drug, but he and the others were used to it and it had less effect on them.

I couldn't wait to find out what it was like to inject speed instead of snorting it. Already I was hooked on having a quick fix. It was amazing. It started to work through my whole body almost as soon as I'd taken the needle out of my arm. In no time at all I was injecting speed and half an amp or heroin on a daily basis.

At first I made sure I used a brand-new needle every time, but once fixing became a daily habit, I became less careful. I injected myself with needles which had already been used, because they were the only ones available in the house. When a friend's girlfriend was unable to find a vein, I took her syringe of speed and injected it into my own arm even though I'd just done a hit myself. I caught Hepatitis B, but, although I was jaundiced and sick for a few days, I soon recovered. It was incredible that I didn't become a regular visitor to the casualty department because, like my mates, I never had a second thought about driving while drugged up to the eyeballs. I had several lucky escapes, but my girlfriend Debbie wasn't so fortunate. When I hit the kerb and sent the bike and both of us sprawling across the road, she ended up with a broken arm and a bad case of road rash.

Somehow I managed to keep this side of my life from my family. When I was around them I tried to be a regular guy and they brought out the best in me, because I wanted to please them. So when James was looking for volunteers to do a sponsored parachute jump I put my name down immediately.

The jump was organized with the Red Devils free fall team at Aldershot. We had training on one day and were due to jump the following day. As I listened to the instructor, I was shocked by all that could go wrong. For example, I learned that if by chance your emergency rip cord was pulled while you were still in the plane, then the chute would get sucked out of the open door and you would be dragged out behind it – but in a straight line which would result in the chute trying to pull you through the side of the plane, not through the opening. The pilot would lose control, since the plane is only a light aircraft, and everyone would die. Another appalling scenario which stuck in my mind was if the chute, which opened automatically, got caught up when you jumped. In this case you'd be towed along outside the plane and you had to put your hands on your head as a signal to the jump master that you were conscious, then he'd cut you loose. This would leave you with one minute in which to eject your main chute and pull the emergency chute. An emergency chute does not give you any control over where you will land, so we were told what to do if we were about to hit the wall of a house . . . or land up a tree . . . or in a lake . . . or on a dual carriageway. Since the field we were aiming for was bordered by a dual carriageway, this particular piece of advice, i.e. don't worry about being hit by a car, just concentrate on how you hit the tarmac, failed to be amusing.

My parents and my sister came to Aldershot to watch me do my jump. I was quite calm as I sat in the plane waiting my turn. Up until the end of the training day we could change our minds and opt out, but no one had. I watched the jump master give the woman who was in front of me a firm push as he shouted, 'Go!' I slid across the floor on my backside and sat in the opening, half in and half out of the plane. Thinking that the jump master was going to push me out, I just let myself go when he shouted. I was caught in the slipstream and it turned me over in a sideways roll, but before I knew it my chute was open and I was floating gently towards the ground. So much for pushing myself away from the plane, spreading out my arms and legs, counting one thousand and one, one thousand and two, one thousand and three, checking my canopy, seeing the thumbs-up signal from the jump master indicating that the jump was a good one. I did and saw nothing of that. Instead I floated through the air gazing at the view and enjoying the peaceful sensation, the perfect solitary quietness.

All this was shattered when a voice shouted directly into my ear, via the one-way radio built into my helmet, 'Put your toes up. Prepare to land. Look across the field. Roll the way you are landing.' I landed competently, and Dad took yet more photos of me. I felt pleased with myself, even though I took a bit of stick for falling out of the plane rather than jumping out. I mightn't have done everything by the book, but I was still better off than the woman who jumped before me. She'd drifted across the dual carriageway and landed up a tree in someone's front garden!

I was intoxicated by the excitement of taking a chance, elated by activities that involved an element of danger. Riding a motorbike provided me with some of the thrills I craved – but a 125cc Yamaha could never give me the buzz I wanted. When I saw a 750cc Triumph Bonnivell in a bike shop in Farnborough, I knew I had to have it. The bike had been registered two years before, but it had never been on the road. There were only eight miles on the clock. The price tag said £2100, but the owner agreed to let me have the Triumph in exchange for my Yamaha plus £200 cash and the rest on hire purchase. I went away trying to work out how long it would take me to get £200 together. I couldn't believe that no one had wanted to buy the bike during the two years it had stood in the showroom. I told my brother-in-law about it and asked if he had any weekend work I could do. He offered to lend me the money then and there, but I wanted to wait until I'd saved up at least some of it. Two days later I went to have another look at it. As I sat astride the bike and admired the black and gold paint work I knew I couldn't wait. I rode the Yamaha to my sister's, asked if I could borrow the £200 after all and was soon on my way back to Farnborough to sign the hire purchase agreement.

I had to wait for two weeks for the paperwork to be processed and I was so impatient that each day seemed to last for a month. Finally the phone call came and I left work early on the Yamaha, very conscious of the fact that this was the last time I'd ride the little bike. The Bonnie was ready for me and my first ride on it was unforgettable. Although I ached to open it up and feel the surge of power from the 750cc engine I resisted the temptation, for this was a brand-new Triumph which had to be run in. I was so proud of my new acquisition that I spent the next couple of days showing it off to everyone I knew.

The feel-good factor that the Triumph gave me lasted for a long time. But it was taking ages to run in, so when my sister asked if I'd like to join her and the family for a holiday in Scotland, I leapt at the chance to put some miles on the clock. I agreed to follow them in their Ford Escort. They had borrowed Timothy's caravan so the maximum speed we could go was 50 mph. Keeping to a constant speed along hundreds of miles of motorway was indescribably boring.

There was also a problem with my drug-taking. I was becoming dependent on speed, especially to keep me awake. I was going to be away for two weeks, and I knew I couldn't take two weeks' supply with me. I consoled myself with the thought that this would be an ideal opportunity for me to take a break from speed. When I left Basingstoke I had only two days' worth of speed and no syringe. I'd have to eat it or put it in a drink or, if I was desperate for it to act more quickly, snort it. But if I used this last method I'd be sniffing like crazy for a while afterwards and I was anxious to keep my drug-taking a secret from Helen and her husband.

The plan was to stop at York for a day on the way to Scotland, then stay at a camp site for a week before moving on. Well before we reached York, my mind was becoming fixed on how I could manage to take some speed without raising any suspicions. I decided to ride ahead of the others, put some distance between us, then pull off the road and lick some speed out of the paper I'd wrapped it in while I waited for them to catch me up. It worked a treat and, after a stop in York for something to eat, we carried on to Scotland.

The holiday was brilliant. Everyone enjoyed it. I was coping well with coming down from speed and, when my sister and brother-in-law wanted a night out, I was happy to look after the children. We spent a day at Hadrian's Wall and I gave in to the temptation to open up the bike on that long straight road. All too soon a fortnight had passed and it was time to return to Basingstoke. I made my own way back. The engine was well and truly run in and I was able to ride like the wind.

Within days I was back on speed, injecting it for near instant effects, and my weekend partying was stretching into the weekdays. Some new friends introduced me to physeptone, a heroin substitute. Mary lived in a flat in Basingstoke, above my grandmother's place. She knew a guy called Schizo Joe who had a large physeptone prescription. He supplied her with the drug on a regular basis. Mary also had plenty of speed in her flat which she bought every two weeks from someone she knew in London. Mary's boyfriend was in prison and I went to see her more and more often, having a hit with her and talking until the early hours of the morning. My girlfriend, Debbie, had hit a bad patch about this time. She became clinically depressed, possibly because she was unable to handle coming down from speed, and was admitted to hospital. I only visited her once and soon after she was discharged from hospital, I finished with her.

I started to travel to London with Mary to get drugs. We had an arrangement with Schizo Joe whereby he sold us as much physeptone as we wanted as soon as he had collected it from the chemist and before he went off to do any other deals. Without realizing it, I was becoming totally dependent on drugs to get me through each day. When James got married I had to find an excuse during the celebrations to absent myself long enough to go to Mary's and have a quick fix of speed. Not long afterwards I noticed a pile of clean clothes carefully arranged in the drawer where I stored my syringes. I realized my mother must have seen them and I felt so guilty that I couldn't even look her in the face. I decided I must leave home immediately.

I moved into a two-bedroom flat, sharing it with a bloke called Hughie. He took anything and everything, didn't go to work but just sat around in the flat playing his guitar. I bought the food and some drugs as my share of the rent. By now I needed a hit of speed early each morning in order to go to work, and quite often I would have a hit in my car during the dinner hour. I'd part-exchanged my Datsun for a Morris 1800, but I'd hardly had time to get used to my new motor before it was written off during a typical weekend of drugs, booze and trouble.

John, Lyn, Albert and I had started drinking in a social club, but after a few pints we decided to move on to Basingstoke town. Everyone piled into my car and we had a few drinks in a couple of pubs, before ending up in the Railway Inn. It was nearly closing time and we'd enjoyed the evening until someone threw an empty glass. It landed on our table. I picked it up and threw it back to the table where it had come from. The landlord told me to leave and wouldn't listen to my explanation of what had happened. He wanted me out. I wanted to give him my side of the story. A bloke walked over to us, grabbed my arm and told the landlord he'd chuck me out. He pulled me towards the door. John, Albert and Lyn followed us out. As soon as we were out in the car park I heard John shout out, 'Oi, mate.' The guy let go of my arm and turned round. 'He's with me,' said John and he hit him full in the face. The bloke slid down the wall. John told me to give him the car keys and we piled into the Morris and screeched out of the car park, hoping to get away before the police were called.

John drove back to the social club where he'd left his car. He turned into the driveway at speed, swung the wheel wildly in an effort to take the car round a sharp left-hand bend, and ran smack into a car on its way out. Both cars were badly damaged, but no one was hurt. The other driver was a woman. Her husband had been following her in his firm's van. We all got out of our vehicles. John and Lyn managed to slip away and collect John's car. The woman driver went to get a paper and pen from her husband so she could take my details. As they were looking in the van for something to write on, John pulled up alongside me and told me and Albert to jump in and hide. He pulled away slowly with Albert lying down by the back seat and me squashed up on the floor by the passenger's seat. The woman and her husband must have been completely bewildered by our disappearance.

We were killing ourselves laughing, and couldn't wait to get to John and Lyn's place for a hit. It had been quite an eventful evening and we needed to sort out a believable story to tell the police when they finally tracked me down. We decided to tell the police that the bloke in the pub car park had been thumped by another man whom we'd never seen before and that we'd left because we didn't want any trouble. As far as the car accident was concerned, we agreed that I would report to the police station in the morning, say that I was the driver but had left the scene of the accident because I had gone into shock following the crash.

The next day I walked into my local police station and made a statement regarding the collision.

Somehow I managed to keep a straight face. Since no one was hurt and the incident had occurred on private land, the police were not interested and advised me to sort it out with the other party. I walked away grinning all over my, face but the Morris was good for nothing but scrap.

I moved to another flat which I shared with Derek, a heroin addict. We rented the flat from Gary who had a well-deserved reputation as the local hard man. He called round once a week to collect the rent and pick up any mail and, as long as the flat was in good order, there were no disagreements between us. Derek was working in the building trade like me. The pay was good but the weather was a problem. As winter closed in we lost more and more days because of the rain. Derek started to get behind with the rent, although he always had money for smack. I told him he should be out looking for ways of making some cash, even doing a bit of shoplifting, instead of banging everything up his arm.

Although bad weather was usually bad news, one day it proved to be extremely profitable. I'd gone into work and hung round like the rest until ten o'clock, to see if the rain would clear. There was no sign of any improvement so everyone else got in their cars and drove off. I decided to have a fix before I left, so I was still on site when a lorry arrived with a delivery of brand new, unmarked scaffolding clips. The compound was locked, no one else was around, so I told the driver to offload the clips by the gate. When he hesitated, I lied, saying the scaffolding gang were on their way. I scribbled a signature on the delivery note and, as soon as he was out of sight, I loaded up my car and drove to Albert's. He knew someone who was on the look-out for any scaffolding and once I'd emptied out my car, we both went back to the site and filled our cars with the rest of the clips. We made £250 each, though according to the local paper the clips were worth £1000.

Back at the flat I offered Derek the opportunity to make some money. I gave him £100 and told him to buy a gram of smack, split it up into smaller amounts and sell them off at £10 a time. He'd be able to make £100 profit. I used £150 to pay the rent and bought some speed to sell on. Over the next few weeks I did quite well dealing speed, but Derek gave me nothing but lies. Every time I returned to the flat, he would be out of his head with his mates and the place was littered with used syringes. I decided to stop paying Derek's share of the rent, and the next time Gary came round to collect it, I told him I'd continue paying my half but in future he would have to see Derek about his payment. Gary didn't seem too bothered, but I was getting really mad with Derek. He'd had the £100 I'd lent him and spent it on smack and proceeded to take it all himself, instead of using it to make some cash. I wanted my hundred quid back, but what rankled with me most was the feeling that Derek thought I was a mug, always available to help him out of a hole. I imagined him and his mates laughing at me behind my back. Derek, I decided, needed teaching a lesson.

I went to see an acquaintance of mine called Gerald. He held a stock of guns and went shooting – all legal and above board. He also dealt a bit of dope. I asked him to lend me a shotgun as I wanted to give someone a warning. Gerald let me have a single barrelled shotgun and a box of cartridges. I went back to the flat and waited for Derek. He came in and slumped in a chair at the table. I walked into my bedroom, picked up the gun and ammunition and sat down across the table from him. As I broke the gun, Derek looked across at me and asked in a vaguely interested tone whether it was an air gun. I slipped home a cartridge and told him that this was a shotgun. Then I pointed the loaded gun at him and asked what was happening with the smack.

Derek's jaw dropped. He realized I wasn't joking and, from my tone of voice, that I was furious. He stuttered out an excuse, 'My mate still hasn't got back from London.' 'Fine,' I said, 'let's go.' 'Go where?' he asked, his voice still trembling with fear. 'We'll go and find your mate and shoot him instead of you,' I replied, getting to my feet. 'But he's got a wife and kids in the house,' stammered Derek. 'I don't really care,' I responded, my voice getting louder and angrier. He had gone a whiter shade of pale and I knew he had got the message, so I said, 'Look Derek, I've had enough of all this rubbish. Either a gram of smack turns up on that table or a hundred quid. It's up to you.'

I walked out of the flat, returned the gun and cartridges to Gerald, told him the gun hadn't been fired and gave him £30 for loaning it to me.The following Friday Derek came in from work and handed me £70. I knew this was nothing to do with the smack but came from his wages, but I took the money, thinking that at least he would suffer by having to go without his usual amount of smack that coming week. Within a few days he should be experiencing some nasty withdrawal symptoms and, with bit of luck, Gary would start pressurizing him for the rent.

That Sunday I was invited to lunch with James and his wife. When I got back to the flat Derek had gone. All our belongings had been stacked up, and there was a note from Gary to say he wanted to see me. I checked through my stuff and discovered that my radio cassette player and my camera were missing. I went straight to Gary's and asked him for an explanation. He told me that he'd called round at the flat and found Derek lying on the floor surrounded by used syringes. He was angry and disgusted and wanted us out. I argued that what Derek did was nothing to do with me and offered to pay the rent until I found someone else to move in. But Gary didn't want to know. Derek had told him about the gun, and he wasn't prepared to listen to anything I had to say. I asked about my missing property, but he denied taking anything of mine. That only left Derek, which surprised me because if you threaten someone with a loaded gun, they're usually too scared to rip you off. Obviously Derek had gone to ground and reckoned that by the time we met up again I would have forgotten all about it. But I had other ideas. I told Gary I was taking possession of all Derek's things and would keep them until he returned my cassette player and camera. Gary had no objection so I arranged to shift the stuff to Mary's. Meanwhile I moved back in with Hughie.

Derek was in a quandary. Gary told him what I'd done and, since I now had everything Derek owned including his underpants, he was desperate to get his belongings back. He vowed he'd not taken anything of mine, but he was afraid to go to Mary's in case I was there. Three weeks passed and, though he phoned Mary constantly about getting his stuff back, Derek still didn't have the guts to come and collect them. In the end I sold his stereo and portable black-and-white TV set, but I never got my cassette player and camera back, nor saw Derek again.

I spent more and more time with Mary. We often took speed together into the early hours of the morning. Usually we went to London to buy it because it was cheaper there than in Basingstoke. Schizo Joe provided us with physeptone. Schizo and I were working on the same building site. He was laying bricks and I was labouring. Every morning Schizo would arrive at work in a terrible state, which didn't improve until the chemist opened and he'd got his heroin substitute. During the morning tea break I'd drive Joe off site and he'd have a hit of physeptone while I took some speed. Joe would always let me have some amps of physeptone which I hid in the car. One day I was out of speed and by three in the afternoon I was desperate. The temptation to have a hit of physeptone became too much and I disappeared off to the car for a few minutes. Although I thought I only took half an amp, the drug affected me more strongly than I could have imagined. I drifted away into semi-consciousness. The next thing I knew was that Joe was banging on the car window. I'd been gone an hour and the bricklayers, now working at the top of the block of offices we were building, were running out of muck. I decided to wash the mixer out and pack up for the day.

When I went into work the following morning, I was given my cards and ordered off the site. I drove round for the next couple of days looking for a job, then, on the day when Schizo Joe picked up his script from the chemist, I parked up behind the shop and waited for him. We might no longer be working together, but I still wanted him to supply drugs for me and Mary. An hour passed and there was no sign of Schizo. I went to the building site, but no one had seen him. I checked out all the other places I thought he might be, then gave up. Mary and I had some speed so we were OK until the following day. She said she'd call at Joe's bedsit on her way back from work. She was still not home when I arrived at her flat, so I waited outside in the car. I'd been up on speed for most of the previous night and needed an amp to bring me down.

At last Mary turned up. She was looking pale and sick. I followed her into her flat and she told me the news. Joe was dead. He'd been found on the concrete stairway outside his bedsit with his head split open. At the inquest the coroner concluded that it was an accident. Joe had taken too much physeptone and had stumbled and fallen.

After eighteen months on the waiting list, the council allocated me a flat on the Buckskin estate. My family gave me some furniture, I bought some second-hand pieces and the place soon looked like home. I was back in work and I found another supplier to take Joe's place. As I moved into my new place in Basingstoke, so John and his family attempted to move out. He wanted to go to Devon, not just because he was a country boy at heart but because the police were watching him. They knew he was dealing and committing other criminal acts as well and they were determined to see him sent down for a very long time. John didn't care who he ripped off. He even stole his next-door neighbour's Triumph. The bloke had spent the best part of a year rebuilding the bike from scratch and he'd only just finished it when John hired a van and spirited it away. He swapped the Triumph for two Hondas, but what gave him the most pleasure was imagining what the bloke's face must have looked like when he discovered his pride and joy had gone.

When I got a £1100 tax rebate, I immediately went to find John. He had the speed and I had the cash. I drove all round Basingstoke searching for him without any success. I ended up at the Nine Saxons pub where I recognized Julie, who was going out with Noel, one of John's friends. She told me John had gone to London to buy drugs, so I settled down to a bit of serious drinking with Julie and her brother. I lurched out of the pub at closing time and couldn't even get my Triumph to start. Julie's brother got it going for me after I convinced him that the cold air blowing in my face would sober me up in no time. I had a spare helmet and offered Julie a lift. She got on behind me and we headed off for John's place. As I drove around the Basingstoke ring road I went to overtake a car. I thought I was in the centre of the road. I could see the headlights of a vehicle racing towards me, and I aimed for the gap between the lights and the car I was overtaking.

The police report stated that a patrol car had started to follow me after they'd seen me pull out of a turning in a dangerous manner. They noted that I didn't slow down on the approach to a roundabout, but went round it at about 60 mph, with sparks flying as the footrest scraped along the tarmac. According to them, when I overtook the car I was only three feet from the kerb on the wrong side of the road. The vehicle coming towards me was a Mercedes van. The driver swerved and mounted a grass bank in an attempt to avoid a collision, but I hit the side of the van and landed up on the road in front of the car I'd been overtaking – driven by an off-duty policeman.

I don't remember too much about that night other than lying on the grass verge, the police wanting to breathalyse me and me swearing at them, then trying to get up. As I put my weight on my right leg, the pain was so agonizing that I collapsed. I regained full consciousness the following day in the district hospital. Every toe on my right foot was broken and the foot itself was fractured. Julie had thirty stitches in a nasty gash in her leg. We spent two days in hospital and even during that brief spell, I arranged for a mate to bring in some speed and puff which we smoked in the day room.

Once I'd been discharged I went to visit John. His house exchange had come through and he, Lyn and Hazel were moving to South Molton. Before he left Basingstoke, John was determined to collect every penny owing to him. One guy didn't have the cash but offered John a replica gun. John took it as payment and stashed it in the boot of his car. That night, when he was driving through Basingstoke, the police pulled him in. They searched the car, found the gun and promptly arrested him. This was just what they'd been waiting for. They got a search warrant and found stolen goods in the house. John was remanded in custody, leaving Lyn and Hazel to move to Devon on their own. When the case came to trial, John ended up with a three-year prison sentence.

When Lyn first moved to Devon, I kept saying I would go and visit her. Albert went to stay with her on several occasions, bringing her back with him to Basingstoke for weekends. Lyn would go to her relations, then Albert would drive her back to Devon on the Monday. One weekend Albert went drinking with a few mates on the Popley estate. They had an argument with some Irish blokes who were also drinking there. The Irishmen were keen to go outside and have a fight. Bruce, one of Albert's friends, told them to sit down and forget it. Their response was to punch Bruce on the nose. With a heavy sigh, he went outside with Albert, to take on the four angry men. They had no idea that Bruce had a black belt in karate. Bruce told Albert to stand back, then he waded in, kicking his opponents in the head. Albert decided to get stuck in too – after all, it was four against one. It was the wrong decision. Bruce accidentally kicked him.

When I heard about it the next day I went straight to the hospital. Albert's skull was fractured and the Irish guys had suffered a shattered jaw, broken ribs and a fractured skull between them. Bruce was always the one to try and stop a fight breaking out, and he had never been in trouble with the police, but with four men in hospital, the police were desperate to find the man responsible for grievous bodily harm. No one grassed: Bruce was safe.

Lyn stayed in Basingstoke that week. I drove her back to South Molton and stayed the weekend there. Albert had told me what a great place it was and he was right. I knew Lyn wanted someone to stay there with her and Hazel while John was in prison, so I said that if I could find someone to look after my flat, I would come and be her lodger. I was prepared to go to Devon for a year, but I needed someone to move into my flat, pay the rent and the bills. Gerald, the guy who lent me the shotgun when I was having trouble with Derek, leapt at the chance. He and his girlfriend, Belinda, were looking for a place where they could be together. They were happy for me to crash out on the sofa every fortnight when I came to Basingstoke to sign on, so I piled my belongings into an old Transit van and set off for the West Country.

Five

Gone West

John and Lyn's house was in a village, a couple of miles from South Molton. It stood in the middle of a row of four, separated into pairs by a central alleyway. Elderly people lived at either end of this little terrace and a couple who were to become good friends, Cilla and Eddie, occupied the house on the other side of the alley. There was a monastery a hundred yards down the road, next to a shop / post office which was run by the monks, and a few cottages. A small stream ran along the bottom of this tiny Devonshire valley and dotted amongst the hills were several farmhouses and smallholdings.

I felt as though I'd stepped back a hundred years in time. Basingstoke was new, raw and busy. Here there was a stillness and a slow, leisurely pace to life. Lyn had made the house a home. She had good taste and an eye for interior design. With an open fire flickering in the living room grate and the smell of burning wood from the kitchen stove, it was easy to imagine being part of an age that has sadly passed. I loved it and understood why John had been so determined to move to Devon.

I arrived towards the end of September. It was the right time of year for magic mushrooms. They grew all around the South Molton area, but Exmoor was the best place to find them. It was only a twenty-minute drive away and it soon became a regular run for me. The first time Lyn showed me where the mushroom fields were, I couldn't believe my eyes. Like a meadow full of daisies, the field was carpeted with mushrooms. Since I didn't know the difference between poisonous and non-toxic mushrooms, I had to keep asking Lyn for advice. We soon had a large bag filled to the brim with mushrooms, but we had to wait until five-year-old Hazel was in bed before we could lay them out on newspaper to dry in front of the fire.

Cilla was an expert on hallucinogenic fungus. She had moved Devon to get away from the hard drugs so easily available in London. Although she occasionally smoked a joint and tripped out on mushrooms, after five years in Devon she was comparatively drug free. I admired her willpower. During my first month there I found it difficult to buy speed, so I started to take magic mushrooms on a daily basis. Every morning I would get up and make a cup of tea, but I would put some magic mushrooms in the pot instead of tea bags. Normally you wouldn't take magic mushrooms or LSD more than a couple of times a month.

After four weeks of taking them every day I was talking in rhyme all the time, seeing things and was generally out of my head 24/7. Lyn began to get worried about me and persuaded me to lay off the mushrooms. Instead I smoked one joint after another and didn't shift from in front of the fire all day, apart from driving to the supermarket in South Molton once a week and taking the dog for a walk. John had had Snapper from a pup. He was a Staffordshire bull terrier with an attitude problem. He disliked Cilla's sheepdog and would chase sheep if he got the chance.

Snapper wasn't the only one in the household causing problems. Hazel was playing up. Whenever Lyn asked her to do something, she would either get moody or ignore her. Hazel wasn't my daughter and my relationship with her mother was purely one of friendship, so I didn't like to say anything, but one evening the usual battle over bedtime really got to me. Lyn kept on at Hazel to go to bed, but she refused and argued back. She was so rude to her mum that, in the end, I gave her a smack across the back of her legs, and told her not to answer her mother back. I warned her that her father would have punished her far more severely if he'd been around. Hazel went to bed in tears and Lyn was shocked at the turn of events. We had a long talk and agreed that things were getting out of hand, but Lyn wasn't happy about me smacking Hazel and decided to talk it over with John on her next prison visit. We realized that we needed to make changes for Hazel's sake. Injecting ourselves with hard drugs had to stop. We resolved to buy as much puff as we could on our fortnightly visits to Basingstoke and make it last when we returned to Devon.

The next time we went to Hampshire, I arranged to visit my parents and Lyn went to Winchester prison to see John. The weekend went well. Albert was now out of hospital and fancied coming to stay with us in Devon. He was suffering from bad headaches and couldn't manage to drive that far, so I drove his car, leaving the Transit parked outside my flat. Albert was happy to go along with our new lifestyle – no hard drugs, just some puff and a drink. He had to be careful in any case because using drugs with the medication he was on could have serious side effects.

A few weeks later I went to talk to John in prison. He hadn't taken exception to my disciplining his daughter, but he wanted to talk about it face to face. As a result of our discussion, I became like a surrogate father to Hazel over the next twelve months, which meant giving her time and treats as well as keeping her in line.

By late November the weather had become miserable. It seemed to rain every day. We were living on a tight budget, but at least food cost us next to nothing – shoplifting in Devon was child's play. Fuel was also free. We used the van and went and helped ourselves. We had a chain saw and whenever we saw a tree that had been felled, we cut it up and took the logs home, sharing them with Cilla and Eddie. As winter drew in, we were on the look-out for something to do in the evenings, other than going to the pub. Cilla, Eddie and their two kids were learning aikido. Lenny, a bloke in his twenties who lived in a van parked in a field at the back of the post office, went with them and Albert and Lyn decided to give it a try. Albert came back from his first session totally enthused. He told me how the instructor could lift a grown man with just two fingers placed under the man's elbows, and that the instructor could make himself such a dead weight that no one could lift him, whatever hold they tried using. I decided to go along, but, since I'd be sitting and watching, not participating, I had a cup of mushroom tea beforehand.

I sat on a pile of gym mats in a corner. As the class started their warm-up routine, the mushrooms began to take effect. Under their influence, seeing the class do their stretches was hilarious, but ten minutes later I stopped tripping completely. I was conscious of sitting alone and feeling left out. I got up, went over to the instructor and asked if I could join in. He took me through the warm-up exercises and demonstrated the lifting technique Albert had told me about. When I left at the end of the session, my mind was buzzing with what I'd seen and, by the time we reached Lyn's, the magic mushrooms had started to work again with a vengeance. What a night!

As the funds continued to dwindle I tried to think of how I could supplement our meagre income. I came up with the idea of signing on both at Barnstaple and Basingstoke. Since Lyn lived more than five miles from Barnstaple, I was able to sign on by post and only needed to present myself at the office once every six months. We agreed to cut back on the number of evenings we spent in the pub and I became an expert at home brewing. Most of our money was spent on travelling. We had to go to Basingstoke every fortnight, and Lyn and Hazel made regular trips to Winchester to visit John. While I was in Basingstoke I would occasionally call in on my family, but I also used my time there to look for anything I could steal. I walked around the estates late at night or in the early hours of the morning, trying the boots of parked cars. It's amazing what you find in car boots and I had a ready market for stolen goods back in Devon.

That Christmas I went out with the Transit and the chain saw and cut down a Christmas tree. Lyn and I spent ages decorating it. We were in the kitchen making a welcome cup of tea when we heard screams coming from the front room. Hazel had got hold of a tube of super glue and, as she tried to stick a picture on the wall, some of the glue went in her eye. We tried to wash it out, but to no avail. The doctor came, but he too could do nothing to help. Lyn and Hazel set off for hospital leaving me at home, worrying about the damage the glue might have done to Hazel's sight, and blaming myself for leaving the glue where she could get hold of it. At last they returned. The consultant had said that Hazel's sight would be unaffected and gave Lyn some special solution for bathing the eye. It took nearly a week before Hazel was able to open her eye again.

A few people came to stay over Christmas, including Lyn's nephew Vince and his girlfriend. They were both eighteen and well into a hippie lifestyle, travelling from place to place and going to all the festivals. I took Vince with me to the Safeway store in South Molton to do a bit of free Christmas shopping. We drove up to the supermarket in Vince's old Morris 1000, and before we entered the shop I gave Vince a cardboard box and told him to walk alongside me. We went up and down the aisles filling the box, then strolled out of the entrance, got in the car and drove off. It was so easy I wondered why they didn't just hand the goods over to me as I walked in!

It was just as simple stocking up on booze. I put on my large trench coat with deep inside pockets – the one I wore when I went mushroom picking on Exmoor – then I wandered into an off-licence. When the woman behind the counter had to go to the back of the shop, I slipped three bottles of wine into the pockets. I bought half an ounce of tobacco and a packet of cigarette papers, and walked out with the bottles clinking merrily against one another. So most of the things we needed for Christmas came free.

The only time I came close to being caught was when I relieved a lorry of two sacks of coal. I had just pulled away when a police car came round the corner and followed my van as I drove home. I was black with coal dust and thinking frantically of a credible story to tell the police when they stopped me. Any explanation I thought up for the state I was in and the presence of two bags of coal in the Transit sounded pretty feeble, but while I was still struggling with my story, the police car turned off down another lane. I put my foot down and, leaving the coal in the van, went indoors and switched off all the lights, keeping watch in case the police came and checked the van. After two hours I was sure there was nothing to worry about, but I still waited until two in the morning before I unloaded the coal in the shed and got rid of the sacks in the woods. Once the evidence had gone, I felt a lot safer.

We spent the New Year with our respective families in Basingstoke. Lyn and I were still off hard drugs and being with our relations helped keep temptation at bay. Back in Devon we experienced snow – snow that made everywhere look pure and white, that didn't turn to a dirty grey sludge as it did in town. I felt as though I was part of a scene from a Christmas card as I trudged up the hills dragging Cilla's sledge behind me, followed by three excited children. We had great fun and only complained when we had to walk the two miles into South Molton to do the shopping because the minor roads were never cleared.

Spring came early and it was good to be out in the fresh air and to see primroses flowering in the hedgerows. It was still my job to take Snapper for a walk, but unfortunately Snapper's behaviour had not improved. One day I let him off the lead in an empty field, not realizing that there were sheep in the next field which was out of sight. I shut the gate and turned round to see Snapper running full pelt up the slope and over the top of the rise. My heart sank. Snapper would only be moving that fast if he had caught the scent of sheep. I ran after him, shouting at him to stop, but I had more chance of stopping a runaway train. I was wearing Wellington boots and the fields were muddy and slippery. By the time I caught up with Snapper he had a sheep up against the fence. I rescued the poor animal, put the dog on the lead and dragged him home. That evening the farmer came banging on our door. He warned us that if Snapper ever worried his sheep again he would shoot him.

As the daylight hours lengthened so our resources grew less. The Transit finally gave up the ghost and couldn't even be used for short runs. This meant we had to pay for firewood and for its delivery. John was moved to Channings Wood prison in Devon so Lyn didn't go to Basingstoke so often. I was still signing on at both Basingstoke and Barnstaple, but with no spare money and no transport, I was left with the choice of hitch-hiking, stealing a car or travelling on the train without a ticket. Most of the time I hitch-hiked, but on the odd occasions when I couldn't get a lift or if the weather was really bad I would steal a car. My Triumph motorbike was still parked up in my brother-in-law's garage. It had been there ever since the accident the year before, and I hadn't made a single hire purchase payment in all that time. The hire purchase company had done their best to contact me, but were told I'd moved. All their letters were thrown in the bin.

It was through another accident that I was able to acquire a new set of wheels. I was on one of my trips to Basingstoke and was spending the day with an old school friend, Bert Lloyd. We were riding push-bikes. I was in front and when I saw an ice cream van across the road I turned round to ask Bert if he wanted one. My front wheel hit the kerb and I shot over the handlebars straight into a barbed wire fence. The barbed wire slashed me across the chest, down the side of my neck and along my left arm. It also left a deep gash in my top lip. Bert took me over the road where there were some houses. He knocked at three doors before someone answered. The woman took one look at me, dripping blood all over her doorstep, and told me not to come in. She fetched a bowl of water and a towel and tried to clean me up, but the cuts were too long and deep, so she drove me to Basingstoke District Hospital. Bert went to tell my parents what had happened. It was when we were chatting about it and having a laugh that I discovered Bert was into motorbikes. I told him about my Triumph Bonnie and he offered to swap his Volkswagen Golf for my bike. The deal was done and as I drove back to Devon I thought that life might be about to get better.

While we'd been without transport Lyn felt really cut off in our little hamlet. She talked about it to John and he agreed that she should put in for a transfer to Barnstaple. Our attendance at aikido had dwindled because it was so difficult to get to South Molton without a car, but now we were mobile again we started to go regularly.

Lenny was progressing well and often practised with Cilla and Eddie. Lyn and I had spent much of the winter sitting in front of the fire stoned and hadn't bothered to practise the moves.

On the Saturday that Lenny was due to take his brown belt, Lyn and I went to Barnstaple to put some cards advertising for a house swap in some shop windows. We weren't able to go and watch Lenny, but Cilla and Eddie went along to support him. On the Sunday Cilla came round in floods of tears. I could tell something was seriously wrong because she was a tough woman who didn't cry easily. I went to the kitchen to make tea, spinning it out to give them time to talk. I even left my cup in the kitchen so I could make a rapid retreat if they were talking about women's problems, but, as I put the cups on the table, Lyn turned to me and said that Lenny had been rushed to hospital after the aikido session and had died a short time later. He was buried in a small graveyard not far from South Molton. It was the first funeral I'd ever attended. We said goodbye to Lenny and threw a sprig torn from a marijuana plant onto the coffin as it lay in the grave.

Soon after the funeral, Lyn was contacted by a couple who were interested in doing a house exchange. They came to look over Lyn's place and liked it. I went with Lyn and Hazel to see their house in Barnstaple. It was great. The living room was large with a bay window, there was a good sized garden at the back and there was a front garden too. Lyn was especially pleased with its location – near the town centre. The paperwork was sorted out, and we packed up and moved on the designated day.

We soon settled into the new house and made friends with a couple of blokes we met in the pub who, like us, were into speed. Michael and Mark were big guys and had a reputation in the town. They didn't start trouble, but if they did get involved in a fight they caused major damage with their fists and boots. They reckoned that I could buy better quality speed on my trips to Basingstoke than was available in Barnstaple. The next time I went to Basingstoke I bought some speed for them which they could cut and sell on. I made my money by charging Michael and Mark a bit more for the speed than I had paid for it, and they made their money by mixing it and selling deals around the town.

I started to look for a job. I could no longer sign on both at Barnstaple and Basingstoke, we no longer had free fuel and the shoplifting was difficult in a town where the supermarket staff were more clued up. Bill, a jobbing builder who employed two brick-layers, took me on. He paid me cash in hand and he didn't mind me taking Fridays off every other week so I could go to Basingstoke to sign on. I was buying speed on each trip. Lyn and I were still not using syringes, but we were taking speed every weekend with Michael and Mark.

At the end of the summer Bill suddenly asked me if I could get some speed for him. I was surprised. He knew that I spent all weekend in the pub and that I wasn't the most law-abiding person around, but he was forty-eight, a family man and wasn't into drugs at all. I had to know why he wanted to start at his age. It was simple. He and his family were moving house and he wanted some speed so he could keep awake all weekend. I promised to get him some from Basingstoke and the following Thursday I set off straight after work. As usual I stayed at my flat with Gerald and Belinda. I noticed the phone had been cut off, so I asked Gerald if everything was all right. He assured me it was and explained that the phone bill was an extra that he didn't need, so I left it at that.

When I went to sign on for the dole that Friday I happened to bump into Georgy. I hadn't seen him in three years. The last time we were together was in a club on the Popley estate. He had a girlfriend at that time called Sally and, as he'd given up smoking, he wanted her to do the same. This often caused an argument. That particular night I passed Sally a cigarette as I handed them around as usual. Georgy snatched it from her and crushed it in the ashtray. Sally was furious. She stood up and threw what remained of her drink down the front of Georgy's shirt and walked up to the bar. Georgy followed her and lashed out, hitting her across the head. About three of us leapt to our feet to prevent the situation from escalating. I reached Georgy first and grabbed his arm. I told him that if he wanted to hit someone, he'd better come outside and hit me. I walked out of the door feeling angrier by the second as I saw again in my mind's eye what Georgy had done to Sally, and how she had looked as the blow jerked her head sideways. I turned round. Georgy was there right behind me. I didn't even think but just laid into him. As he went down, I kicked him in the head, then I walked back into the club shaking with anger.

Albert was there that night and he went out to see how Georgy was. We didn't usually fight among ourselves and my violent reaction had shocked everyone, including myself. Albert took Georgy home to clean him up and I gradually calmed down. I had a couple of drinks with Sally then offered to take her to Albert's house. Albert wasn't in, but his wife Carol said we could wait for him. Time passed and there was no sign of Albert and Georgy. Carol said we could stay as long as we wanted, but that she was going to bed. That night I slept with Sally as we waited for her boyfriend to turn up.

Three years on and Georgy told me how he had left Basingstoke to live in Bournemouth and had just finished a stretch in jail. I told him about Devon and he said he'd like to come down and stay. After we'd signed on we took some speed and went for a drink together. On the Sunday night I said I'd ask Lyn if he could come for two weeks and promised to give him a lift both ways if she agreed.

I gave Bill some speed at work on Monday morning. I told him it was good stuff and warned him not to take too much of it at a time. When I went into work the next day, Bill was looking shattered. He'd decided to try out the speed before the move. He slipped some into the cocoa he and his wife had as a bedtime drink and neither of them had had a wink of sleep. He dared not tell his wife what he'd done and luckily she put their insomnia down to the excitement of moving house.

The following Saturday, I drove to Exmoor to pick the first of the season's crop of magic mushrooms. On the Monday I asked Bill if he'd like to try them and he said he would. That evening, I boiled up a heap of mushrooms that I'd picked and dried out over the weekend, and made up a flask of mushroom tea. The next day I offered Bill a cup when we stopped for our morning break. The other bricklayers weren't in – there were only the two of us. Bill drank a full cup and accepted another half cup. I had made the brew pretty strong so that he would get a proper trip even if he didn't drink a whole cup. I hadn't foreseen him drinking a cup and a half!

We went back to work. Bill was building a spiral staircase in yellow bricks – a tricky job at the best of times. I went to the mixer to make sure we had enough muck knocked up. As I tidied up round the mixer I started tripping on the mushrooms. After a while I was fit enough to check up on Bill. Walking into where he was building the staircase was like entering a yellow void. He couldn't focus properly on the brickwork and I was no use to him, so by dinnertime we packed up and went home.

Lyn had said that Georgy could come and stay for a fortnight, but when I went to Basingstoke to pick him up, there was no sign of him. Some weeks later he turned up unannounced in Barnstaple. We sat down together in Lyn's house and had a few joints and sampled my home brew. I had become quite an expert. I made forty pints of double strength beer at a time and had fifteen gallons settling nicely in three five-gallon barrels. That night Georgy and I went to the pub. We talked about the old times and what we used to get up to when we were at school. When the landlord shouted last orders, Georgy decided to take a couple of bottles of beer home.

As we walked back to Lyn's still reminiscing, the conversation turned to the evening when Georgy had thumped Sally. I admitted that I'd slept with Sally that night and the next moment Georgy hit me full in the face with a bottle. The bottle smashed and the broken glass slashed my nose and face. The force of the blow knocked me off my feet and as I lay on the pavement Georgy leaned over and spat out the words, 'I loved her.' I scrambled to my feet and went after him. He turned and started to walk backwards never taking his eyes off me. He had blood on his face and I thought it must have come from me. I didn't know how badly I'd been cut, all I knew was that I wanted to put things right between us. 'Look Georgy,' I said, 'I don't blame you for being mad. I'm not going to have a go at you, so let's leave it at that.'

Georgy nodded his agreement stiffly and allowed me to walk alongside him. We tried to flag down a taxi, but when the driver saw my bloodstained face he refused to take us. By the time we reached Lyn's we were best of mates again. Lyn was shocked when she opened the door and saw the state I was in, and even after I had cleaned myself up she and Georgy wanted me to go to hospital. I refused, but the next morning I woke up with my face stuck to the pillow. As I pulled my face away from the pillow the wounds opened again, so I had to go and have them stitched. I was left with a deep scar on my nose to remind me of that night out with Georgy!

Two days later I was back to work. Georgy left after two weeks. At the end of November Lyn heard that John had been given parole. He would be home just before Christmas. I was planning on spending Christmas with my family in Basingstoke and I had bought presents for everyone.

A few weeks before Christmas, I phoned my father to tell him I'd be coming. He said they were going to Timothy's over Christmas so would probably see me in the New Year. Timothy had only ever invited me to his home once in all the time I'd been back home, so I rang my younger brother and asked if we could get together at Christmas, but he too was going to Timothy's. I told him that if the family didn't want to see me at Christmas it was obvious they didn't want to see me at all. Ten years would pass before I saw them again. I took some of the presents back to the shop where I'd purchased them and got a refund, I kept some and gave the rest to other people. Lyn invited me to stay with her and John, but I couldn't do that. John needed to be on his own with his family. I stayed in Devon until the 23rd so I could say hello to John, then I went to my flat and stayed with Gerald and Belinda. Belinda's parents ran a pub a few miles outside Basingstoke and we all went there for Christmas dinner. It was fun and I congratulated myself on having spent two consecutive Christmases out of prison. I returned to Devon to see in the New Year with Lyn, Hazel, John and his parents.

I was thinking of moving back to Basingstoke now John was back home, but when I mentioned it to him he insisted that I stayed on. Over the next few months John settled into his new life. I enjoyed his company. Some nights we'd go to a deserted beach where we could scream at the wind and the waves. We drove around the area and I took him to see where I picked mushrooms in the autumn. There was good pub up on Exmoor which sold proper scrumpy cider which made you drunk just smelling it. While we were there I told John about the beast of Exmoor. No one knew what sort of animal it was, only that it killed sheep and roamed the moor. Nobody had been able to catch it – even the army had tried and failed. One day I was on the moor picking mushrooms when I came across the remains of a sheep. The bones had been licked clean and lay scattered across a torn fleece. I had been in that very field the day before. By the look of it I'd just missed an encounter with the beast itself!

As time went on I began to consider putting in for a flat exchange so I could stay permanently in Devon. I was forced to take action when Gerald rang me to say that the police had raided my flat, and he was on the run because they'd found drugs and a gun. The next day I told Bill at work that I needed some time off and I set off for Basingstoke. I soon discovered that the drugs the police had found only amounted to an eighth of an ounce of puff and the gun was an air rifle. I knew that Gerald was dealing drugs, but I was surprised that he had gone on the run for such a small amount. Then I started to look through a pile of bills. There was a red one from the gas company demanding £200 and threatening to cut off the supply and, as I sorted through the paperwork, it became clear that Gerald had not paid any bills for ages. Every bill was in my name, and now I wanted to see Gerald before the police got him. It wasn't difficult. Albert told me he was staying in the pub with Belinda's parents. He offered to come with me once he heard that Gerald had run up bills in my name to the tune of £700. We found Gerald and got £100 off him and a promise that he'd pay the rest over the next few months. I told him I was moving back into my flat and he'd have to shift his stuff out. Thanks to him I had to stay in Basingstoke and sort out the mess – or lose the flat.

Six

No Escape

Gerald had run up an unbelievable amount of debt in my name. I no longer regarded him as a friend, but following the bottle incident, Georgy and I had become great mates again. Georgy, Albert and I started to have nonstop drink and drugs parties at my flat every weekend. We called them 'binges' and they would kick off with Georgy and I driving to Bournemouth, where we had contacts who supplied us with top quality speed called pink champagne. Neither of us was working at the time so we'd siphon some petrol out of the tank of a parked car on the Thursday, drive to Bournemouth on the Friday and fill up there for the trip back to Basingstoke.

One week we were looking around Bournemouth for a likely car to provide us with free petrol, when we noticed one with a coat lying across the back seat. We could see the corner of what looked like a wallet sticking out of a pocket. I had a big bunch of car keys on me, but none of them opened the door, so we cut the rubber out of the side window at the back with a Stanley knife, removed the window and helped ourselves to a wallet containing £300 in cash and a stack of credit cards. We went straight back to our supplier and did a deal with him. We gave him the credit cards, then set off for home with acid, speed and dope plus the £300. It was going to be some party!

Quite a few of us ended up at my flat that weekend after doing the rounds of the local pubs. Georgy and Albert were there of course, together with Albert's friend, Ricky, plus another bloke, Ray, who'd recently been released on parole. I'd only met Ricky once before this particular Saturday night when he'd been drinking with his common-law wife, Charlotte, at the same pub as me. The binge at my flat was going well, but at about one in the morning the booze ran out. I decided to drive round and try and buy some drink from an hotel. Ricky offered to come with me and we used Albert's car, a Vauxhall Viva, as it was the least likely to attract the attention of the Old Bill. We had no luck with the hotels, so Ricky suggested we go to his Mum's as she often kept a few beers in the fridge.

When we got there we found only one bottle of lager, so we stayed and shared it between us. Ricky's Mum was still up. She was baby-sitting for Charlotte and Ricky. As we chatted to her, the phone rang. It was Charlotte ringing from her flat in Reading seventeen miles away. Ricky took the call. Charlotte was screaming down the phone that there was a guy in the flat trying to rape her.

We raced to the car and headed for Reading. When we got to the estate, Ricky told me to drop him off outside his flat. It was nothing to do with me, he said. He'd sort it out on his own. I told him we'd stick together. The chain was on the front door, but Ricky shoulder barged the door, broke the chain and ran into the front room. A man was sitting in an arm chair. Charlotte was on the other side of the room. There was blood under her nose. Ricky lifted the man bodily out of the chair and punched him again and again, then dropped him heavily onto the floor. As he lay there I kicked him in the chest and stomach. We stopped beating him up only because we were afraid that the noise might wake the neighbours who would probably call the police.

It was, by now, half past two in the morning. Ricky reckoned the bloke was drunk and he wanted him sober, so he could feel the pain when he had another go at him. I agreed to take him back to my flat. I drove with Charlotte sitting beside me, while Ricky held the man down in the back. I told him it was going to be his last ride and this set Charlotte off. She hung over the back of her seat, trying to hit the bloke over the head with the heel of one of her stiletto shoes. Ricky had to intervene and I turned off into the country roads, in case anyone saw what was going on in the car.

When we arrived at my place, I went on ahead and told the others what had happened. Ricky dragged the bloke into the flat and we tied his hands behind his back with some wire flex and dumped him in the bedroom. Back in the living room we cracked open some bottles of barley wine which we'd brought back from Charlotte's place and indulged in some more speed. Albert was ferreting around in the kitchen cupboards and found a jar of hot chillies that Gerald had left behind. He thought a stomach full of chillies might sober our 'rapist' up, so the two of us went to the bedroom and force-fed our victim. We left him there, spluttering and gagging.

A few minutes later he stumbled into the living room mumbling about water. 'He's trying to escape,' I said sarcastically and I punched him so hard in the face that he fell over. Charlotte dropped to her knees beside him and yanked his trousers down. 'Look at the big, hard rapist now,' she jeered. The contents of the man's trouser pockets spilled onto the floor. Albert rooted through them and picked up a wallet and a small tin containing Valium. He extracted a cash-point card from the wallet and asked the bloke what his pin number was. He could only mumble an incomprehensible reply. 'He's so out of his head he can't feel anything,' said Ricky in disgust. I went to a drawer in the sideboard and took out a Webley 175 air pistol and a handful of pellets. 'He'll feel this,' I said, and having loaded the gun I pointed it at his chest and asked him for the pin number. He told me, then added that there wasn't much on the card, but that he had another card at home. 'How much have you got on that one?' I asked. 'About £500,' he replied. 'That's not enough,' I responded and I shot him in the chest from a distance of about two feet. Ricky punched him a few times, then we lost interest and carried on drinking and taking drugs until five in the morning.

As it became lighter, we decided to get the bloke out of my flat. Ricky and Georgy dragged him to the car then drove off into the country a few miles from Basingstoke. They bundled him out, stripped him naked, beat him with a bamboo cane and left him in the middle of nowhere. On their way back to my place, they dumped his clothes. Later that morning Albert tried the cash card but only managed to get £10. I thought no more about it until the following morning when I noticed a blood stain on the carpet. I tried, unsuccessfully, to get rid of the stain with salt water. By this time we had all gone our separate ways, and hadn't made any plans to get together to work out what we'd say if any one of us got pulled in by the police.

Two days later Albert, Georgy and I were smoking dope and playing music in my flat. It was late in the evening and Albert's youngest son was asleep in the bedroom. Albert and his wife were divorced and he only had access to his children once a week. Georgy and I had done some acid, but Albert had confined himself to smoking some grass because he wanted to keep his head straight while he had his boy with him for the night. There was a knock on the front door. A guy I knew from the pub was on the doorstep wanting to know if I was interested in some stolen jackets. Georgy went down to the car with him to have a look at them, leaving the door on the latch.

I was just starting to come up on the acid I'd taken and I was getting into a Pink Floyd album when the needle became stuck. I got up to move it and heard a police radio in the room. I turned towards the sound and saw five CID officers piling into the living room. There were more police wearing flak jackets in the hall. I thought it was a drugs raid so I sat down quickly on the sofa, and while the police started searching the flat and asking questions, I was busy slipping the acid tabs out of my pockets and into the holes in the sofa. They picked up the bong that was on the table and found a box full of unused syringes. I told them that everything belonged to me. Meanwhile Albert noticed the cash point card lying on the sideboard. He palmed it and slid it down his sock. I managed to hide the tin of Valium in another hole in the sofa. One of the officers picked up the car keys and asked whose they were and while Albert was telling him they were his and giving a description of the car another policeman called out triumphantly, 'I've found the gun!' At this point I realized that this was not a drugs raid but to do with the guy we had done over forty-eight hours ago.

Albert was arrested and the police took him and his son away, dropping the boy off at his mother's on the way to Reading police station. They kept me in the flat until they had searched it from top to bottom. They found all the evidence they were looking for – the gun, pellets, the wire flex, the blood stain and the card. They managed to miss the dope I'd stashed in the kitchen and the acid and Valium in the sofa. I was arrested and taken to Reading. On the way the lights and the acid took their toll on me. When one of the officers said, 'It's all right, we know what it's all about,' I mistakenly assumed he meant that he knew the guy had attempted to rape Charlotte and I thought that he must have a record for rape, so I responded with, 'It was lucky for him I only had an air gun and not a shotgun, or else I'd have blown him away.'

Albert, Ricky and I were all held in the same cell block at Reading police station, so we were able to talk to each other quite easily. Ricky told me that he and Charlotte had been arrested at their flat that morning. They had kept quiet about us, but the guy we beat up must have said that there were others involved. What did surprise us was that Georgy wasn't in the cells with us. He'd only left the flat a couple of minutes before the police arrived. I supposed that he and the bloke with the dodgy jackets had seen the police vans turn into the car park and had escaped. I was still tripping on LSD and found the whole situation hilarious. I told the others that I'd admitted to shooting the bloke and they were horrified. Albert said tripping had loosened my tongue dangerously. He advised me to keep my mouth shut when they came to interview me and only to ask for a solicitor. While he talked to Ricky through the hatch, I spent an hour making different patterns with the speckled paint on the walls in my mind's eye. When an officer took me to the interview room, I told him I couldn't be questioned because I was on drugs, but I did want a solicitor. A solicitor wasn't available until the next morning, but they insisted on calling in a doctor to check me over.

The following day we heard that both Georgy and Ray had been arrested and taken to Basingstoke police station. None of us made any comment during our first interviews. More information filtered through to us. The bloke I'd shot had had an operation to remove the pellets from his chest. After he had been dumped, he'd walked naked for a mile before reaching a house, where he got help and called the police. While we waited for further questioning we decided on a strategy. I would admit to the shooting; Ricky and I would admit to beating the guy up; we would try and get Albert, Georgy, Ray and Charlotte off and hoped that Ray and Georgy would say nothing to the Basingstoke police.

I spoke to my solicitor, but by eight that evening we still hadn't been charged. Georgy was transferred from Basingstoke and was locked up in the same row of cells as us. He said they'd released Ray without charge, which was good news. The questioning went on, but time was running out for the police. They had to charge us or let us go. It happened large scale. All of us were charged with kidnap, false imprisonment and robbery. Ricky, Charlotte and I were also charged with GBH and I had possession of a firearm while on a firearm ban, and using a firearm to cause ABH added to my list of charges. Charlotte was released on bail, but we men were remanded in custody and taken to Reading jail. We spent two weeks appearing in court, applying for bail and being refused and sorting out with our solicitors what we should plead to each charge. They persuaded us to plead guilty to kidnap and false imprisonment, because we couldn't deny that we had taken the bloke from one flat to another. We agreed between ourselves to say that we had no plans to keep the man in my flat, but had taken him there to give him the opportunity to sober up so we could find out the truth of what happened with him and Charlotte. Unfortunately, the story would continue, two of us had been drinking heavily and things got out of hand, so Georgy suggested taking him away in the car for his own safety.

As we fine-tuned our story, we discovered details which put a different slant on the whole incident. Charlotte had directed the police to my flat. She had been having an affair with the guy we'd beaten up while Ricky had been in prison. That night she'd bumped into him in a pub and invited him back to her flat. For some reason the evening turned sour and she phoned her mum to say the bloke had tried to rape her. I still don't know to this day where the blood on her face came from.

After two months on remand we went to the magistrates' court for committal. We were sure that ultimately we would be dealt with by the crown court but hoped that some of the charges would be dropped. All the charges against Georgy were dropped and he went free. Ricky, Charlotte, Albert and I were committed to appear in the crown court but, apart from Albert, we were no longer charged with robbery. The charge of GBH against me was dropped, as was that of kidnap in Albert's case. We went back to Reading prison. Charlotte was released on bail.

Over the next few weeks we had to decide whether to ask for judge and chambers bail. It is really only worth applying for if you are sure you will not end up with a prison sentence. As the only evidence against Albert was the cash card hidden in his sock, he decided to go for it. Ricky and I knew we would be sent down so we were content to stay on remand as the time we served would be deducted from our sentence and we benefited from more privileges being on remand – for example a visit every day and having tobacco sent in.

Two months passed and during that time we saw very little of Georgy, even though we'd agreed that if any one of us got out, he would make sure the others were OK for drugs. Although Gerald owed me money for the flat, he only came to see me twice with some puff. I managed to get hold of the acid and puff that was stashed in my flat. I gave my keys to a couple of women Albert and I knew, and told them where to find it. They smuggled it in during a visit, but as the weeks went by, the visits became less frequent, and we were surviving on the few ounces of tobacco that friends sent in.

Things got worse with the news that Charlotte had been arrested again, this time for robbery with another guy. Ricky was furious, and when this bloke was committed to Reading prison on remand, Ricky beat him up on the landing. Ricky was moved to another prison and Charlotte was sent to Holloway. Her involvement in an attempt to rob a corner shop was going to make it more difficult for us when we went on trial. The court wouldn't feel very sympathetic towards a woman whom we wanted to portray as a helpless victim of attempted rape, when it became known that she'd made the masks for a robbery, stood by the shop door while the shopkeeper was threatened with a knife, and then escaped in a stolen car.

The weeks on remand dragged on. Albert spent every spare minute painting. He'd enjoyed art at school and now that he was able to devote all his energies to it, he became really good. I found a profitable way of using my time too – selling his paintings for tobacco and the odd joint. This worked well, until the day I went to collect the tobacco payment from a prisoner who'd taken one of Albert's pictures and sent it as a present to a member of his family. I went into his cell.

The guy who owed the tobacco was sitting on the top bunk with his legs dangling over the edge. His cell mate was sitting on the bed opposite. When I asked for the tobacco, he replied with a sneer, 'What are you going to do if I don't pay?' I could tell there was going to be trouble, but I didn't stop to think. I grabbed his legs, pulled him from the bunk and punched him in the face. Then I took a punch in the side of my head from the other guy. As I turned round to hit him I received a blow to the stomach which doubled me up. A knee came up, smashing me in the face, and I tried to move back towards the door, protecting my face at the same time. Then the riot bell went off and I heard the sound of feet running along the landing. I got another kick in the mouth before the screws arrived. They took me to hospital and the others to the block. I had lost a tooth, had a black eye and a bruised cheek, but was otherwise fine. I'd given the other bloke a black eye, but his cell mate was unhurt. I told the governor that it was an argument over a roll-up and assured him that it was over, finished and forgotten. Albert was willing to carry it on, but I told him it wasn't worth it. I'd lost a fight, he'd done a painting for nothing, we might or might not win round two, but we'd certainly end up in the block.

Then Albert heard that he'd been refused judge and chambers bail. This was particularly bad news for him as he was concerned about his children. Karen was living with another man and had moved into a house in Tadley, just outside Basingstoke. One day Albert had a visit and came back looking desperately worried. He told me that there'd been a fire at the house in which Karen and the children were now living. The old wood burner in the kitchen had blown up, luckily while the children were at school. No one was hurt but the house was badly damaged, and he was anxious about what would happen to the children. He was relieved when their grandparents agreed to take them in until the house became habitable again, but the wait for the trial seemed endless.

We'd been on remand for nine months before we were given a date for the hearing. Before the trial took place, we heard that Charlotte had admitted that she had lied about the guy attempting to rape her. False accusation and attempted robbery were not going to gain her the sympathy vote, and would adversely affect the jury's opinion of the rest of us.

As we stood to hear the sentences, I guessed that mine would be between three and seven years. Albert got a six-month sentence for stealing £10 with the cash card. As he'd already served nine months on remand, he was released. Ricky got two and a half years. The judge said he'd been provoked as he was Charlotte's common-law husband. There were no mitigating circumstances when it came to me. According to the judge I had involved myself in the matter, had taken the law into my own hands and acted as judge and executioner. He gave me a four-year prison sentence. As for Charlotte, he said, she was the cause of all the trouble. Had she not lied, none of what followed would have happened. She got four years too, which pleased me: the judge was right when he put all the blame on her.

I was allocated to the Verne prison. It is a category C establishment situated on an island off Portland. There's a naval base at one end of the island and a closed borstal at the other end. Being a C category jail meant the regime in the Verne was relaxed and easy-going. I had my own room and a key. There were no bars on the window and inmates were allowed to have a rug, curtains and bed linen sent in to make their rooms feel more like home. They were free to walk around the prison and take a bath whenever they wanted. I settled in very quickly and soon made friends with a guy on the landing below called Greg Hope.

Greg and I used to club together with our canteen and buy some puff between us. Albert visited me regularly, bringing in whatever he could afford, which was usually quarter of an ounce every fortnight. Mary came once a month and always brought some puff with her, as well as items for my room. I was working in the carpentry shop and Greg was doing a car mechanics course, so between us we had access to all we needed to make hash pipes and bongs.

I'd been in the Verne for a few months and was sharing a joint in my room with Greg, when a new inmate walked past with another bloke from my landing. When they smelt the joint they stopped and asked if we could spare them some dope until they had a visit. It was a difficult decision. We only had one sixteenth of an ounce, which would last us two or three days. Craig Shark, the older of the two blokes, claimed that he was due a visit that coming weekend if not before, but in the end, we told him and the other guy, Sammy, that we didn't have enough to do a deal. However, they would be welcome to sit down and share a couple of joints with us.

We chatted and smoked for a time. Sharky was about fifty, a businessman type, quite tubby, with grey hair and glasses. I found I distrusted him almost as soon as he opened his mouth. Sammy was young and slim, and just to look at him you would know he was into drugs and anything else that was on offer. The two men had met the day before when they were both moved to the Verne. Sharky boasted that he was finishing a nine-year sentence for possession of a ton of cannabis. This struck a false note with Greg and myself. We knew that a lot of sex offenders and lifers were sent to the Verne when they were coming towards the end of their sentences and Sharky's story sounded like a cover-up for what he was really in jail for.

Sharky picked up on our suspicions and showed us his charge sheets and police reports. He explained that he had been shipped out of Channings Wood prison, because his visitors had been caught on the gate with a large amount of drugs on them. The prison authorities had their suspicions about him and arranged for the police to stop and search his visitors. He was sent to Shepton Mallet, a B category prison, and now, much to his delight, to the Verne. He was ready to take the chance of getting two and a half ounces smuggled in on one visit. Again Greg and I had our doubts. We finished smoking our sixteenth of an ounce and acknowledged that whatever Sharky was or wasn't, he could certainly smoke dope! Two days later Sharky had his visit and came back on the landing with two and a half ounces of puff.

Over the next year or two I got to know Sharky really well. He was a professional con man. He swindled drug dealers as well as businessmen and sold fake perfumes on the market in his spare time. He didn't care how he made money as long as he made it. Every night, he and Sammy, Greg and I would sit in my room and smoke. Early each morning Sharky and I would go down and see the night watchman to get a jug of hot water, then we'd share some coffee and a couple of joints before breakfast. The screws ignored the smell of dope. As long as there were no outbreaks of violence connected with drug taking, they didn't get involved. We had a constant stream of inmates coming to us for deals. We did deals for everything from a pot of jam to a watch. There was only one commodity Sharky wasn't interested in dealing in and that was money. This surprised me and the other cons, as most people who arranged for drugs to be brought in wanted to deal in cash, so their visitors could make a profit. Then they went away happy and keen to smuggle in more drugs on the next visit, whilst the prisoner had a supply of drugs which doubled in value once they were inside the prison walls. An inmate who couldn't get drugs brought in from outside would ask his visitors for money so he could buy them from a fellow con.

Six months down the line Sammy was due to go on home leave. This was a great opportunity to get a big parcel in. Sharky arranged for Sammy to meet a mate of his, Kenny, once he was out. Kenny was a young bloke who ran a rave club called Beyond Therapy. He had experience of doing fairly big drug deals involving kilos of weed and solid dope like rocky. Rocky was a particular favourite in jail. It was easy to hide up your bum and to weigh using a pencil, ruler and penny coin. It also went further when you rolled a joint and didn't smell quite as much as other forms of marijuana. Arrangements were made for Sammy to go to London and meet Kenny on the last day of his week's home leave. Thinking that we were soon going to have an abundance of dope, we stopped rationing ourselves and smoked like it was going out of fashion.

One of our preferred methods of smoking dope involved a powdered milk tin made into a pipe. We called the finished article 'Captain Marvel'. One advantage of using the 'Captain Marvel' pipe was that minute particles of the dope and oil built up on the inside of the tin and could be scraped off with a razor blade and made into a nice joint.

As Sammy enjoyed the first few days of his home leave our supply of puff decreased rapidly, but we knew we could borrow some dope from a couple of inmates until Sammy returned with our parcel. We borrowed half an ounce and had already smoked half of it by the night Sammy was due back. We were expecting him to bring in at least five ounces. The amount was restricted only by how much he could put up his backside and the quantity he could swallow. We had the scales set up in Greg's room and we kept a close watch on everyone coming over from the gate. Inmates returning from home leave usually arrived between five and seven in the evening. Anyone arriving late was taken straight to the block and had to see the governor the following morning. Unless they had a very good excuse, they ended up losing some remission or spending a few days in the block. If a prisoner wasn't back by nine o'clock he was assumed to have absconded.

There was no sign of Sammy as the seven o'clock deadline came and went. We started to get worried. At half past seven Sharky phoned Kenny, only to discover that Sammy had not been to see him. Something had gone seriously wrong. We spent the next two days trying to get a visit from Kenny in the hope of uncovering some clue as to what had happened to Sammy. The guy from whom we'd borrowed half an ounce of puff was getting anxious. It was OK to borrow on the strength of a parcel coming in, but if that parcel didn't materialize everything went pear-shaped. The person who lent us the puff had promised deals to other cons based on us giving him half an ounce back plus a little extra. They too would have made further deals so that within a short space of time everyone in the prison seemed to know that something had happened and rumours were rife. We finally found out that Sammy had joined some other blokes in an armed robbery which had gone wrong. He was caught while he was still in the get-away car and was being held in a local prison. We never saw him again.

Kenny managed to smuggle in half an ounce which we gave to the guy we owed. We had to borrow a further quarter ounce from someone else to fully repay him, so he could carry on dealing without getting into debt. Another visit from Kenny and one from Albert set us right again and we continued to make deals and invite different people into my room for a smoke, a chat, to do business or to set up on what Sharky called a 'mumble'. This meant laying the groundwork so that we could con them when they, and we, were released. What with inviting people in and giving them the odd joint now and then, we were pretty well liked in the Verne and never encountered any trouble.

During the eighteen months the three of us spent together, Greg Hope's grandfather fell ill and was taken into hospital. His condition was critical so Greg was given permission to visit him, but because he had so much of his sentence still to serve he didn't qualify for home leave or a day's parole. He had to be escorted to the hospital by a prison officer. Despite this obstacle, Sharky saw the visit as an opportunity to bring some dope in from the outside world, so we formed a plan. Kenny would arrive at the ward during Greg's visit and introduce himself to the officer as Greg's social worker. He would have a few minutes' chat with Greg and slip him the drugs. If they were allowed to go somewhere private or out of sight, well and good, but if not, Greg would have to go to the toilet at some point so he could hide the drugs up his backside.

With the plan formulated and dates and times set, it was party time again. Although we thought we had learnt our lesson with Sammy, we still managed to smoke nearly all the dope in our possession before Greg went to the hospital. By the time he went to see his grandfather we had only enough left for one night. Our expectations were sky high as we waited for Greg's return. Nobody else knew our plans, we hadn't borrowed any dope from anyone and we were looking forward to having a good smoke.

One look at Greg's face when he returned brought us back down to earth. Kenny had not turned up at the hospital and we had only enough puff for that evening. Sharky phoned Kenny, who admitted that he'd arrived ten minutes too late at the hospital, so we set about borrowing from others until we got a visit. Then came news that Greg's granddad had died and our hopes were raised again. We could have another go, as Greg was going to be allowed to attend the funeral. This time everything went to plan and he came back with the goods.

Time drifted by with little to differentiate one day from another. We got some enjoyment from winding up a prison officer who was bent on catching us with drugs and seeing us severely punished. He caught us smoking cannabis once, but the governor considered we had only committed a minor offence and fined us. This particular screw was furious, and even more determined to expose us as evil drug-taking villains. We started to go to other house blocks to smoke when this officer was on duty, but on one occasion we were in my room and decided to have a laugh at his expense.

We lit up a joint, blew smoke along the landing and put on some loud music – all of which made him think he had a good chance of catching us at it. But, as he crept along the landing holding his keys so they wouldn't make a noise, we got rid of every scrap of evidence of drugs, which included mopping the floor with some crushed roll-on deodorant to mask any smell. He tapped on the door and flung it open with a look of triumph on his face, only to encounter three innocent roommates and the sweet smell of deodorizer. Although such incidents brightened up the prison day, we knew we had to be careful. The officer might get his own back by insisting that the police searched our visitors at the gate. This had happened to Sharky when he was in his last prison and we couldn't afford to push our luck too far.

Around this time I received a visit from Georgy. He'd not been to see me since I'd been in the Verne, and when I inquired after him, both Albert and Mary said he'd left Basingstoke to go and live in Bournemouth, but they knew no more than that. It was, therefore, a surprise when Georgy wrote to me from a Southampton address asking for a visiting order. I sent the order and waited impatiently for visiting day, thinking Georgy might bring some speed with him as we'd done a lot of speed together in the past.

The day came and I sat down facing my old friend across a table and watched him for a sign that he was going to pass me something illegal. It didn't happen. Georgy just chatted as though we'd met in the street. I became more and more impatient. 'What have brought me then?' I hissed at him. 'I hope it's puff 'cos that's what I'm into mainly.' Georgy looked me straight in the eyes and said he hadn't brought me anything. I was mad. 'Why have you come then?' I asked ungraciously. 'You've been inside, you know it's a waste of a visiting order if you don't score. What's the matter with you?' Georgy shifted in his chair.

He looked slightly uncomfortable. 'There's nothing wrong,' he assured me, 'but I've come to tell you something.'

Then it all came rushing out and what Georgy told me left me speechless. He'd stopped taking drugs and was worshipping regularly at a church in Southampton. He burbled on about being washed clean and born again. I switched off and let him talk while I thought about what I could salvage from this extraordinary visit. In the end I got five pounds off Georgy, which was hardly worth the risk, and I told him that if he wanted to see me again, would he make sure he came with Albert as I needed some puff brought in on every visit. Georgy left. I never saw him again. I bought some tobacco with his fiver and forgot about him.

Although we were shut away from the outside world we soon heard about a new drug that was doing the rounds at raves and acid house parties. It was called ecstasy or 'E'. We thought we'd get some ecstasy in and give it a try. Mary said she could get hold of some and, on her next visit, she slipped me four E's. I was expecting some puff as well, but each pill cost as much as an eighth of an ounce of puff, or more if you only bought a couple. At the time E's were selling at £20 a tab and an eighth of an ounce of puff cost £15. Needless to say, Mary could not afford to buy both. Greg Hope, Sharky and I each took a tablet and exchanged the fourth one for an eighth of an ounce of puff. We didn't sleep a wink that night, but weren't impressed enough with the buzz to try and get any more in.

With less than a year to serve, the three of us were looking forward to our release dates. I had completed a bricklaying course and was working on an outside party, which gave me the opportunity to bring in parcels for myself and other prisoners. We hardly ever had to have a drug free day. I applied for home leave and it was granted six months before my discharge date. I had arranged to stay with Mary for my home leave. She had moved out of her flat and had taken out a mortgage on a house in Oakridge Road. The home leave board were happy for me to stay in her spare room.

I was excited about getting out, but that didn't affect the plans I made to bring drugs back into the Verne. They were for myself, Sharky and Greg, plus two ounces for a guy called Malcolm with whom we were doing good business. Sharky and I covered every angle. On the last night of my home leave I would go and stay with Kenny in Tottenham Hale. Kenny would give me as much puff as I could bring back. Sharky advised me to fast the day before so I would be able to swallow as much puff as possible. He was going to phone me at Kenny's to check that all was going well. Malcolm arranged for his wife to meet me in a hotel car park on the evening prior to my return to prison, and he gave me details of the car's number plate. Mary would drive me there and Malcolm's wife would give me two ounces of puff and fifty pounds. The money was my payment for smuggling in the drugs for him.

I arrived in Basingstoke on the first day of my home leave and went straight to see my probation officer before I'd even had a drink – I'd made that mistake before! I spent the next few days going out and about with either Albert or Mary, and I came across Gerald who gave me a couple of ounces of puff and few quid to spend. One night Gerald took me to a casino. We had a meal then played roulette and blackjack. I had a great time and thoroughly enjoyed losing £250 of Gerald's money. It didn't bother him. Gerald's drug dealing had grown from selling half ounces and ounces to buying kilos of puff and selling it on to small dealers in and around Basingstoke. Although he was well wedged up, he still hadn't given me the full amount he owed me on the flat and I'd not forgotten that he was the reason I'd had to leave Devon, in order to sort out the mess he'd left behind him when he went on the run.

While I was on home leave, I went to my first rave. Having an E at a rave was far better than in prison and I was impressed by this 'designer drug' and would have liked to try it again, but all too soon the week was nearly over and I had to prepare for my return to the Verne. I had an ounce and a half of puff from Gerald, which I'd cut up and wrapped ready to swallow during my last night at Kenny's flat, and I'd acquired another two ounces from Malcolm's wife. The rendezvous had gone as planned, but she didn't have any cash for me.

When I arrived at Tottenham Hale tube station, Kenny's common-law wife was there to meet me and take to me to the flat. Within minutes of meeting Kenny, I was rolling a joint and marvelling at the amount of weed spread out on some newspaper on the floor from which, Kenny told me, I could help myself. It was very different from the careful rationing I was used to in prison and I made full use of my host's generosity. Sharky phoned and I told him all was going well apart from the missing £50. I described what was available from Kenny, using a code in case the prison phone was being tapped. Sharky asked me to bring back half an ounce of weed and three ounces of Lebanese. In all I had seven ounces to take back.

On the morning of my return, I got up early and started swallowing the puff. At first I swallowed the packets with some custard, but when I began to feel full, I replaced the custard with drink. I still had about an ounce left to swallow when it was time to leave to catch a train back to Portland. Rather than leave it behind, I took the ounce with me to take on the way. I downed the rest of the dope with a few beers on the train. Having not eaten much for nearly two days I was soon feeling the worse for wear. I staggered up to the gate and was wobbly on my legs as I checked in to reception. It was against the rules to drink while on home leave and I could have been taken straight to the block, but the officer gave me a chance. He said if I could walk to my house block without falling over, he'd ignore my condition.

I made it and, as soon as the coast was clear, Greg, Sharky and I sorted out some of the leb for Malcolm and, after a couple of goes on Captain Marvel, I was ready for an early night. The next day nature took its course and Malcolm got his two ounces, although we did have words about the missing money. In the end Malcolm's missus admitted that she hadn't paid me, so we charged Malcolm quarter of an ounce for bringing the stuff in. I felt really pleased with myself for having successfully brought so much dope in. It was quite an achievement, but the fact that we didn't run out of puff two weeks after my return was noticed by the prison officer who was out to get us.

Just after breakfast one morning, Greg and Sharky were in my room having a cup of tea before we went off to our places of work, when in walked this officer with another screw from reception who was carrying a kit box. The kit box was used for the personal possessions of a prisoner who was being transferred, and the sight made us all very nervous. They picked on Sharky. He was going to be sent to another prison without notice. They accompanied him to his room to supervise his packing.

I knew Sharky would be trying to think of a way of getting hold of some puff to take with him, so when the reception officer came back to my room and said Sharky had left a book in Greg's room, I knew that meant Sharky was hoping we'd be able to get some puff to him before he left. I went to Greg's room and found the biggest single lump there. It weighed in at about quarter of an ounce. I picked up a book, went back to my room and collected my coat, then walked into the room where Sharky was waiting. As I entered I pulled on my coat, slipping my right arm down the sleeve. The puff was clenched in my right hand. I was holding the book in my left hand. I moved between Sharky and the screw, turning my back on the latter and hoping to obstruct his view. 'Here's the book from Greg's room,' I said, offering it to Sharky, and at the same time I pushed my right hand through the sleeve and shook him by the hand. I pulled my coat on properly and left with a casual, 'See you then.'

I was hardly through the door when the screw jumped on Sharky. He held him below the chin, preventing him from swallowing the puff which he'd transferred from his hand to his mouth. He was forced to spit it out and, at that moment, the reception officer hit the riot bell. I was on my way down the stairs and kept going as a crowd of officers ran past me. I wanted to make it to the outside working party and I did. Nobody radioed to the gate to stop me and I thought I was in the clear.

All day I wondered what had happened to Sharky, but when I came back through the gates at dinner time and saw the security officers waiting just inside, alarm bells began to ring in my head. They pulled me to one side and searched me but found nothing. I tried to play the innocent, but they ignored me and took me to a cell where they strip searched me. Again they found nothing. Without a word they marched off, locking the door behind them and leaving me to get dressed, as I tried to work out what was going to happen to me. I found out the next morning. I was being charged with possession of a class B drug and with supplying a class B drug to another prisoner. They had transferred Sharky, but no one knew where he'd gone. After thinking about the evidence the officers had against me, I decided to plead not guilty when I appeared before the governor.

Although I was in solitary confinement, I could still shout up to someone in the house block and they could throw things into the exercise yard which separated the punishment block from the house block. My exercise periods were always taken at the same time, so Greg would throw a bit of puff into the yard just before I came out. I picked it up and smoked it back in my cell with great care and some trepidation. If the officers got a whiff of any dope in the punishment block they would be straight in, turning the cell inside out, looking for the gear.

When he heard the evidence against me, the governor decided that he would not deal with my case but put it before the board of visitors. Two days later I was transferred to Channings Wood prison. Greg had shouted across the yard to me that Sharky had been sent to Dartmoor, so he had the worst of it, being banged up in a B category jail whilst I still benefited from the more relaxed regime of a C category prison. Despite what had happened to us, I still hoped that Greg would be able to get me at least an eighth of an ounce of puff to take to Channings Wood.

With my personal possessions packed and signed for, I waited with two prison officers for the taxi which would take me to Channings Wood. It arrived and I walked towards it, only to be stopped momentarily by Greg, who handed me a newspaper saying, 'There's something to read on the way.' 'Thanks, see ya,' I responded, trying to feel where he'd hidden the puff in the paper. I located it in the middle and it felt as if it was as much as quarter of an ounce. I knew that somehow I had to hide it up my backside before I went through reception at Channings Wood. I couldn't swallow it because I had nothing to drink. As we clambered into the back seat of the taxi I managed to retrieve the puff from the paper and push it into my pocket. I had to move fast because I was expecting to be handcuffed to one of the officers during the transfer. As it was, they didn't bother with the cuffs for the short drive to Verne's reception area. I was worried that they would search me before I had the opportunity to get the puff out of my pocket, but it didn't happen. I was ordered to enter a cubicle and change out of my prison uniform into my own clothes. I had plenty of time and privacy to hide the puff, then after signing a few forms I was handcuffed, climbed back in the taxi and was on my way.

As soon as I was settled in my cell at Channings Wood, I wrote a coded letter to Sharky telling him that I'd been charged with possession and supplying drugs to another inmate. We corresponded very rarely so as not to draw attention to ourselves and the plans we had for when we were finally released. Within twenty-four hours of my arrival I'd found someone I could do a deal with, been caught smoking a joint and put on report. The following day I managed to hoodwink the governor and got away with a severe warning about the prison's zero tolerance of drugs.

During my induction week I decided to apply to work in the kitchens. It would be a new experience for me and although the hours could be irregular, the pay was good – around £5 to £7 a week. Also kitchen work was said to be a bird killer – it kept you so busy that the time flew by! My job came through and I joined all the other kitchen workers on the kitchen landing. This had definite advantages. We were earning good money so there was no shortage of tobacco, and there were ample supplies of food and yeast available from the bloke in the bakery section so we were able to make hooch.

Six of us, including Tom the landing cleaner, held regular parties on the landing. We would make up batches of four gallons of hooch at a time in five-gallon plastic milk bags. While the hooch, hidden in a clothing box under the bed, was brewing Tom made sure the cell was regularly mopped with prison issue roll-on deodorant to mask the smell. We were given one stick a month; Tom used one a day on the floor! Once the hooch was ready, we put it in a store cupboard and inmates working in the kitchen could help themselves. We had an unwritten law that no one would get drunk whilst in the kitchen. It wasn't hard to comply because we were always so busy: there was little time to stop for a drink and we knew that, at the end of the shift, we could smuggle some back to the wing and enjoy it at leisure.

The governor thought he was running a tight ship – I suppose he was in a way! His officers turned a blind eye to our home brewing, even when we used one of the tea urns as a vat. I often thought of Sharky, knowing he was far worse off than me. It was difficult to get drugs into Dartmoor and a long way to travel for visitors. Whereas the screws in Channing Wood left you alone most of the time, in my experience prison officers in Dartmoor were quick to use violence at the slightest provocation.

Sharky and I were summoned to appear before a board of visitors at the Verne. As I entered a large room near reception to wait for the coach, I saw Sharky in amongst the other prisoners who were being transferred on that New Year's day. We managed to get handcuffed together and had plenty of time on the journey to get our story straight for the board. It was decided that I would plead not guilty and deny handing Sharky anything other than the book. He was going to plead guilty and say that he already had the puff and was trying to hide it in his mouth. Unless anybody had evidence to prove that I had had the puff in my possession, I should be found to be innocent of the charges against me. Sharky hoped the board would treat him leniently in respect of his admission of guilt to being in possession of drugs.

The members of the board seemed taken aback when they heard our pleas. We were returned to our cells and were called in separately. I went first. Two officers gave different accounts of how I handed over the drugs to Sharky. One said I'd hidden the packet up my sleeve and tried to slip it to Sharky when I deliberately interposed myself between the two of them. The other said I passed over the drugs in a handshake. With such blatant inconsistency, it was no surprise that I was found not guilty. Sharky was found guilty and lost sixty days remission. The officer who had always had it in for me informed me that, now I'd been found not guilty, I could finish my sentence in the Verne. I looked at him long and hard. 'No thanks,' I said, 'I'm a lot happier where I am.' Back in Channings Wood, the weeks sped by and my discharge date soon came round. In no time at all I was out of the gate and boarding a train to Basingstoke.

Seven

Double Dealing

As soon as I arrived in Basingstoke, I went straight to Albert's place on the Popley estate. After a few drinks, I told him about the plans I'd made with Sharky to take a couple of grand off Gerald, who still owed me money on the flat. Albert was sceptical. Like me, he knew from experience that much of the talk in prison comes to nothing once you're out. I could understand why he had his doubts, but I wanted him to be in on the scam, so that we could both get our own back on Gerald. Albert had done plenty of favours for Gerald in the past and yet Gerald, now shifting large amounts of dope, had done nothing in return to help Albert. He even charged him for the puff that he brought me when I was in prison. I was convinced that Sharky meant what he said and would go through with our plans, but, because of his reaction, I didn't bother to tell Albert about all the other victims we had set up while we were inside.

I moved in with Albert and before long I ran into Gerald. I made out I was pleased to see him and, in the course of conversation, told him that I could get puff for him from London at a price that was about £200 cheaper than he was paying. He was impressed. He offered to pay me £50 for every kilo I bought for him. I agreed, and he gave me the money to go and buy a kilo. When I returned with his kilo, Gerald was delighted. The dope was quality at a really low price. He wanted me to go and get some more right away. I said I would on two conditions – that he always paid me up front and that I collected the drugs on my own. He couldn't agree quickly enough.

Gerald was hooked and I couldn't wait to tell Sharky about it, but he was still in Dartmoor with about a month left to serve. I decided to visit him and smuggle in enough dope to see him through the final weeks. I managed to buy a second-hand car and arranged to visit John and Lyn in Devon, before going on to Dartmoor the following day. I spent a couple of days with my old mates and discovered that John knew Sharky. They'd done time together in Channings Wood. John was keen to visit Sharky with me and wasn't bothered about me taking some puff in. The visit went well. The officer in charge was watching someone across the room so I was able to pass the dope to Sharky before he'd even sat down. Sharky remembered John and we talked about people we knew and about dealing. John told Sharky that he was buying a kilo of puff at a time and selling it on in four-ounce lots to drug dealers around Barnstaple. Sharky offered to put in a word so John could buy his dope from Kenny. The visit ended on a high note as Sharky and I looked forward to getting together on the outside at last.

It was only when we were back at John's place that I found out that Gerald was John's supplier. He went to Basingstoke to see him every month. I warned John that I was doing a pay-back job on Gerald and that I would let him know when not to buy from him. I could have told him not to deal with Gerald from that moment on, but I didn't want Gerald to get any inkling that something wasn't quite right.

Sharky was released and went to Holland for a week to celebrate his new-found freedom. By this time, I had hit the back of a parked lorry and written off my car but I wasn't bothered. I was too excited by the thought that very soon I was going to have my revenge on Gerald. I told John not to buy anything from Gerald and I told Gerald that I was going to Holland with another guy, and that he could have part of a shipment of one hundred kilos that this bloke was setting up. Ever since my release, Gerald had been trying to persuade me to introduce him to Kenny or Sharky. He was going to meet Sharky very soon and it would be a meeting he would never forget.

I joined Sharky in Southend. From there we phoned Gerald, saying we were in Holland and needed to know how much dope he wanted to buy. He collected orders and cash from everyone he knew. He had £6100 to spend. We met up and went through Gerald's list with him. Pleased to have met Sharky at last, he willingly handed over the money. We left with his cash and I promised I'd bring the stuff back from London as usual. I wonder how long he waited before he realized that I wasn't coming back – ever.

Instead of going to London we went to Albert's flat. We checked there were no phone numbers or addresses that could lead anyone to us, then shut the door behind us. Another chapter in my life was over. I never saw Albert again. I put his keys through the letterbox and Sharky and I set off for Southend.

We were soon settled in a three-bedroomed house with a guy called Ben. He worked in London and did the rounds of the clubs at weekends. Sharky and I invested some of Gerald's six grand in watches to sell on street corners. We got in with a bloke Sharky had known before he went to prison – Tommy Sellers. Tommy had years of experience selling fake goods such as perfume, gold and watches in markets and on the streets. We all went to Epsom together where Sharky and I shifted the watches while Tommy sold the gold.

Sharky was soon buying large quantities of goods from warehouses and selling them on to market traders and to a swag shop in Oxford Street, run by a London firm. I went out selling with Tommy most days and became used to earning regular sums of money. Occasionally I pulled in extra cash from scams organized when I was in jail with Sharky. Dog End was one of our victims. He'd been in the Verne with us and, after we'd been in Southend for a while, I contacted him and arranged for him to come from Wales to meet me at Waterloo station, where I promised I'd have a kilo of dope for him at a very special price. Dog End turned up with his father and I told them to give me the money and wait in the coffee shop. I explained that Sharky was parked up outside the station with the bag of dope. I'd fetch it and place it on the floor between us. Dog End could pick it up and check out the contents in the gents while I stayed with his father. We went to the coffee shop, but they weren't happy about handing over the money, so I left them there and reported back to Sharky. He went to see them for himself, and whatever he said convinced them because he came back to the car with the cash, and we drove away celebrating getting something for nothing!

Sharky spent much of his time working in the Oxford Street shop with Howard, who also lived in Southend. The shop was stacked with boxes of goods and, once it was full of punters, the doors were closed and the goods auctioned off. The items were all high street returns, so a customer might be lucky and walk away with a hi-fi with only a scratch on it, but he could end up with a microwave oven that didn't work at all. Dissatisfied customers who took the time and trouble to come back were only allowed to exchange their purchase for another item. They never got their money back. Sharky did the books for the shop and bought the stock. I delivered the stock in a three-ton lorry twice a week, and Sharky supplied me with stuff to sell on the streets and at car boot sales. On my way to the shop, I dropped off some of the load at a garage we rented in Wickford, so we had supplies for nothing and Sharky fiddled £500 every time he did the shop accounts.

My life had changed radically. I spent much of my time with people who had loads of money. I didn't go to the local pubs, but spent most evenings indoors getting totally stoned. If I went out, it would be to a restaurant with Sharky and Kenny. Sharky started dating a woman called Pauline. They were both divorced and had children from their previous relationships. Her teenaged son, Phil, was on the verge of a criminal career so Sharky moved in with Pauline and took Phil under his wing. He soon had him working in the Oxford Street shop. In his spare time Phil and a couple of his mates broke into any place that looked a good bet or an easy touch.

For a time I stayed on with Ben. He was a decent bloke, but he brought home some strange people from the clubs. They'd stay the night and disappear Monday mornings. When Pauline offered me the spare room at her place, I jumped at the chance. We were a very mixed household. There was Sharky aged 50, Pauline 40, daughters Valerie 22, Anne 20, and Claire 9, son Phil 17, and me, the lodger, 37. Valerie had a flat in Southend and Anne had a studio flat in London but stayed with Pauline most weekends. Everyone was involved in crime and/or drugs.

Soon after I moved in, Sharky got his hands on a few hundred half-empty perfume bottles. Always looking for a nice little earner, my bedroom was turned into a perfume factory. Using a syringe I topped up the bottles, repackaged them and sold them with Sharky at Wembley market where Sharky's friend, Bruno, had a permanent pitch. Tommy Sellers taught me a lot about selling. He would sit on a box with five different well known perfumes in front of him, and a stack of plastic carrier bags at his side. There'd be two or three women planted in the crowd who'd show a lot of interest in his sales pitch. He'd pass some perfume to them to try out and they'd appear really impressed with it and rush up to buy at the end of his spiel. Later, in the car park, they'd give back the perfume and were paid for their performance. People actually believed he was selling Chanel and other top names and were amused when he said they were stolen goods. In fact the perfume wasn't stolen, just cheap! Every time I took a fresh box of perfumes to Tommy, I took away the empty box with the money. If the police pulled him in, which happened at Crawley, I nipped back to the car with the perfume and the cash and drove home to Southend.

With the street selling, the Oxford Street shop and the drugs scams, the money was rolling in. Sharky bought himself a Saab 900 turbo, but I stuck with older, cheaper motors: I was stoned so much of the time that I was regularly involved in accidents. In one year alone I wrecked seven cars. As Sharky said, I 'killed cars' every time I went out in them. Unsurprisingly I became uninsurable.

As Christmas approached, Sharky suggested that the two of us and Pauline went away for a break. It wouldn't be for long, as there was a small fortune to be made in the run-up to Christmas, and Sharky had to be back in time for the shop to re-open after the holiday. He couldn't allow anyone else to cover for him in the shop, as they might find out how he was fiddling the books and robbing the stock. We decided to go to Jamaica and booked the flights and hotel. I worked extra hard so I'd have plenty of spending money. The excitement was building. I'd never flown further than the Channel Isles before and that was when I was a kid, and the second and last time I'd been in a plane had been for the charity parachute jump. There was no time to have any injections done and I had to pay someone £50 to sort me out a passport, but I couldn't wait to celebrate Christmas in Southend then fly out to the West Indies.

The Christmas period brought me an unexpected bonus. Phil and a couple of his mates had an office job lined up. They asked if they could use my car and if I'd give them a hand. They were certain that there was a wall safe in the office, which we could take out and carry off the premises. Once we were well away, we could open it with the aid of a crowbar and club hammer. I agreed to help them out. I wasn't worried about my car. It was only worth £200 and, because of the number of accidents I'd had, I'd long stopped putting cars in my name. The job went like clockwork. We each took £200 from the safe then dumped it, so I had a fat wad of cash in my wallet when we set off for Heathrow airport on 30 December 1991.

After an hour's delay we boarded the plane and landed eight hours later for refuelling in Orlando. Another two hours' flying and we reached Montego Bay Airport. What a contrast it was with Heathrow. We got off the plane straight onto the runway, the airport buildings looked like a large aircraft hangar and the customs check was just a joke. As soon as we stepped outside, we were surrounded by men offering us everything from cannabis to a can of beer. We bought some of both these essential commodities to make the bus ride to our hotel in Runaway Bay even more enjoyable.

I was knocked out by the hotel. My room, next to Sharky and Pauline's, was huge with two double beds in it. It looked out over the swimming pool to the beach and the sea beyond. Doors led out onto a balcony and that's where I sat enjoying a joint and letting the unpacking go hang. Sharky came round to get the bag of weed off me, and warned me not to leave any signs of dope smoking in my room for the cleaner to find, or we'd have the hotel security on our case. I shared another joint with Sharky and Pauline, then changed into shorts and a T-shirt and went exploring.

There was one main road, more like a wide country lane with a grass verge but no pavement. As I walked along it, listening out for any vehicles, I was stopped by locals who wanted to sell me dope. They were very friendly, but I quickly learnt that if I showed any interest at all they became very pushy, determined to get a sale. Each one of them tried to convince me that he had the best weed in Jamaica. It was only the normal collie weed, but it was far better quality than was available in England. I managed to get away from these eager salesmen of Jamaican home-grown and back to the hotel in time to have a joint before dinner.

This was the first time I'd ever stayed in a hotel, and that evening I made a bit of a fool of myself. It began when I was refused entrance to the dining room because it hadn't occurred to me to change from my casual gear into something more formal. Dressed properly, I was able to join Sharky and Pauline and soon made my next faux pas. The food was laid out buffet style for guests to help themselves. I was used to queuing up and collecting my food in somewhat less luxurious surroundings and, rather than watching what the other guests did, I followed prison procedure and filled a tray with everything I wanted to eat instead of helping myself to one course at a time.

Then came the cocktails. I drank and enjoyed my first one. There was plenty of fruit juice in it and it was full of flavour and easy to drink, but when I'd finished it I asked the waiter to bring me one with more alcohol than fruit juice. Sharky told him to bring me a Zombi. The name should have been warning enough, but I didn't want to back down now I'd made a stand about wanting something stronger, so I reiterated the order and a Zombi was placed before me. Tentatively I took a sip through the straw. My taste buds shrivelled. This was alcohol with a dash of fruit juice. By the time I'd finished one Zombi I was sliding off the chair into oblivion. Somehow I managed to find my feet, and staggered out of the dining room onto the beach hoping the fresh air would sober me up. I collapsed on the sand and when I woke up waves were lapping round my feet. It was just as well there was no such thing as a high tide in Runaway Bay! At three in the morning I finally made it to bed.

We spent the next day doing deals with the locals and arranging to buy some good sensimillia from them, then we lay on the beach and smoked a few joints. By the time we'd finished our evening meal, the guy who'd promised to go and pick up the dope we wanted still hadn't shown up. We decided to go to the bar over the road and wait for him there. The bar was typically Caribbean. It had a straw roof held up by wooden posts but no walls, and the tables and chairs were made from logs and lengths of timber. By the time we'd had a couple of drinks, a guy called

Bradley arrived with the sensimillia weed. It was quality and after we'd smoked a joint of it we asked if they had a bong we could use. They called it a chalice and it was made out of a coconut and bamboo cane. I was so stoned when I got back to the hotel that I could hardly stand.

After that night, we hired Bradley both as our driver and our go-between with the drug dealers. He knew exactly where to get the best dope. Bradley had an old Ford Capri which we had to bump start every ten miles. Only suitable for the scrap heap in England, it was in better condition than many of the cars on the island. He was friendly, didn't drink and never got upset. He usually earned £7 a week. We paid him £5 a day. I started going around with him at night, so Sharky and Pauline could have some time to themselves.

Bradley and I only ran into trouble once. It was late at night and we were about to enter the Rooftop club. A Range Rover pulled up and two armed men jumped out. They loosed off a round in the direction of some people sitting a table set in amongst the bushes. I was back in the car like greased lightning, but Bradley trotted out his usual comment when anything happened – 'It's no problem, boss.' 'What do you mean, no problem?' I replied urgently. 'There's two blokes toting guns over there. Let's get out of here.' 'They're police,' he drawled, 'just firing a warning shot in the air before they arrest the cocaine dealers.' Somehow his casual attitude reassured me and I got out of the car and followed him into the club. Everyone behaved as though nothing had happened, so I got on and enjoyed myself which was never difficult in Jamaica!

After nearly two weeks in Bradley's company, I found I was no longer bothered by minor setbacks. When one of the car tyres started to shred its rubber, he hacked it off with his machete and drove on. I offered to buy a new tyre for safety's sake, but his optimistic attitude was unshakeable – 'It's no problem,' – and it wasn't. The tyre didn't puncture and we continued to racket about the island. On another occasion a catch gave way, and the bonnet flew up with such force that the hinges bent. Unable to see a thing, Bradley stood on the brakes then calmly got out, wrestled the bonnet back into position, found a bit of string, tied it down and carried on.

We had not planned to take any weed back to England with us, but a couple of days before we were due to leave, we changed our minds. We decided it was worth smuggling some dope back, but as Sharky had been in prison for drug offences and was more likely to be stopped and searched by customs, I opted to be the carrier. The dope would be mainly for our own use and we wanted the best. Bradley took us to Three Mile Island, Bob Marley's birth place, where we bought some top grade weed. The day before we left I asked Bradley to buy one hundred condoms for me, and he and a friend joined me in taking all the stalks out of the dope, compressing it into small balls and wrapping them up individually. I was still trying to swallow the last of the balls of dope when the bus arrived to take us to the airport. I managed to get the remainder secreted up my backside, then boarded the bus. I cleared Jamaican customs, but

I knew that Heathrow wouldn't be so easy and I had to endure a ten-hour flight without having anything to eat in case it made me want to go to the toilet. I needn't have worried. The customs officers at Heathrow showed no interest in me or my luggage. Anne was waiting for us and she drove us back to Southend in her brand new Ford Fiesta.

It was cold and wet, but memories of Jamaica warmed me up as I went back to work on the streets and in the markets. By spring 1992, we had organized our next big con job. A new stain remover was being extensively advertised on Channel 4. It cost £7 and came in a tube inside a box rather like toothpaste. Sharky and Tommy Sellers had thousands of cardboard boxes bearing the product's name printed, and filled them with plastic bags containing the cheapest washing powder they could procure. We sold three for a fiver. It sold like hot cakes. As it was a new product customers thought there hadn't been time for any fakes to be made, so they believed they were buying the genuine article but for £16 less than the advertised price. People were queuing up to buy it. On top of this I still had the other goods filched from the Oxford Street shop to sell, and I was often involved in extra earners in the evenings.

One night I was out for a walk when I spotted a jet ski on a trailer parked in someone's driveway. My van had a tow bar but it had broken down. I went to see Valerie's boyfriend. He could find a buyer for the jet ski, but he couldn't help me steal it as he didn't own a car. In the end we borrowed Anne's motor. It didn't boast a tow bar, but we had a length of rope and thought we could tie the trailer to the Fiesta's bumper. We parked at the bottom of the road and walked up to the driveway. To my surprise and delight, the trailer wasn't chained or padlocked to the tow bar. We detached it and pulled it down the road by hand. It started raining, and we pulled the hoods of our coats down over our heads, trying to obscure as much of our faces as possible. Nobody was around, but I felt quite vulnerable, tying a trailer containing a jet ski to the bumper of a Ford Fiesta. I hoped it would stay attached during the journey to the garage where Sharky kept the stock we nicked from the shop.

I locked the trailer and jet ski safely away and congratulated myself on seeing an opportunity, seizing it and making a nice little packet without too much sweat. The rain was still falling as I drove back to Southend along the A127. I came up behind a cluster of three cars and pulled out into the fast lane to overtake them. As I passed the second vehicle, I noticed that a road works lorry, with warning lights flashing, had stopped up ahead in the fast lane. I put my foot down to get past the third car quickly, but the driver accelerated as soon as I got level with him. I swore and braked so I could drop back behind him – but it was too late. I'd run out of time and I was almost on top of the lorry. I stood on the brakes, the wheels locked and I skidded helplessly into the back of the lorry. The lorry driver saw it all. He was standing on the central verge about to cone off the area. His vehicle wasn't damaged, but the front of Anne's car was severely rearranged. I gave him a false name and address, got Anne's car taken to the scrap yard then broke the news to Anne that she must report her car stolen. She was fully insured, but I felt I had to give her the money I'd make from the jet ski to cover the hike in her insurance premium and the hassle I'd caused her.

With my Toyota box van stuck in a garage waiting to be fixed, I had to use a hire van or lorry for the deliveries to the shop. One day I picked up the goods in my hired lorry from the warehouse, unloaded 'our share' in the lock-up and had time to kill before going to Oxford Street. Deliveries there had to be made after the shop closed at 5 pm. I decided to have something to eat at Pauline's house, and was interrupted by a couple of Phil's friends who were looking for him. Phil had been working in the shop that day, so I suggested they came in the lorry with me since they might catch him before he left. I wasn't being kind – I could do with the extra hands to roll my joints on the journey and help unload at the shop.

We arrived at the shop at 5.30 pm, but no one was there. I phoned Howard on his mobile and got back into the lorry to wait for him. I climbed into the passenger seat and rolled a joint from some of the last of the Jamaican weed. I'd parked at a bus stop and, just as I was enjoying my smoke, a policeman approached the lorry. I slipped the joint into my left hand and held it down by the door. I was explaining that we were waiting to unload, when the policeman caught a whiff of my joint. He wanted to see what I was smoking, and wouldn't accept my answer that it was only a herbal cigarette. He told me to get out of the lorry, but I clambered over to the driver's seat. Using my body to block the policeman's view, I picked up the rest of the Jamaican weed, wrapped in cling film, from next to the ash tray. I promised I'd drive round the block until I could unload, but by now the officer was losing patience. He opened the door and pulled me out by my legs. I turned and jumped so he had to let go of my legs, but he obviously thought I was going to attack him because he called for assistance on his radio. He tried to grab my hand, but in the ensuing struggle I managed to throw the weed over towards the front of the lorry. I didn't see where it landed, but I hoped the Old Bill wouldn't be able to find it. Within seconds, so it seemed, police cars came screeching to a halt from all directions and I was held up against the lorry, my hands cuffed behind my back. They held me there while they searched the ground around the lorry. Just when I thought my luck was in, one of the officers noticed a small piece of cling film sticking out of one of the holes in the hub cap.

I was charged with possession, but released once Howard had signed for the £50 bail. The two lads were released without charge. We returned to the shop, unloaded the lorry and drove back to Southend. Two months later I was fined £25. I paid it gladly knowing that I was extremely fortunate not to have been charged with assaulting a police officer – often the result of a call for assistance – or having the contents of the lorry impounded and checked for stolen goods.

We still talked about Jamaica and how much we'd enjoyed it there, so much so that Anne decided she wanted to go. She asked who else would like to come, and I said I'd love to but it depended on my cash situation. Sales of the fake stain remover were still going well and Sharky was able to put more work my way. Sharky had opened a small warehouse in Southend and a shop in Crawley, so there were plenty of deliveries for me to do. Phil's two mates were working with us, as was Adrian, who had his own car and sold some of the stock from our lock-up.

The Crawley shop was set up differently from the one in Oxford Street. It had 'Closing down' signs emblazoned across the windows all the time. Scratched and broken goods were sold as ex-display items. Twice a week, Tommy Sellers set up a table outside and shifted the £10 watches and other bits and pieces. I was making money steadily, so I told Anne I'd definitely come with her to Jamaica and Adrian said he was up for it too.

Within days of making this commitment, my Toyota van let me down big time. It made horrible knocking sounds and smoke poured from under the bonnet. The big ends had gone and the garage said it was irreparable – I needed a new engine. I wasn't prepared to break into the £700 I'd saved for Jamaica, so I asked Sharky for some of my share of the money we'd made from conning the drug dealers. He told me it was all tied up in the Oxford Street shop and the warehouse, so I couldn't have it. My immediate reaction was that he was jealous because he was too busy to come with us to Jamaica. When I worked it out, however, I realized that my share of all the scams we'd been involved in since coming out of prison added up to around £15,000, and so far I'd only taken £1000, which I'd spent on clothes and a car. I'd lived on the money I'd made from selling on the streets and doing deliveries. For the first time I began to think that not only was Sharky conning drug dealers and the people running the shop, but me as well. I bought a Metro for £200 so I could cart around the stuff to sell on the streets, and told Sharky that I wouldn't be able to do the deliveries for him any more.

Despite my doubts about Sharky and my money, I continued to live with him at Pauline's place, and we enjoyed our evenings smoking puff together. During the day I worked with Donny selling the stain remover. We got on well, even though he was only nineteen and I was thirty-seven. I didn't feel that much older than him, and often went to raves with him, Phil and his mates. Kenny was still running his club and, if Sharky went, he would sit in the VIP part but I'd go with the lads, do some E's and have a good time. I also went out with the youngsters some nights to do break-ins, usually offices but always somewhere that offered easy access. We kept whatever we stole at Donny's flat until we were able to fence it, and Donny also let me store the remaining stock of stain remover there.

The flat had seen better days. The walls, windows, curtains and furnishings were all stained a dirty yellow with nicotine. Donny lived with his Dad, who was hooked on heroin. His addiction had started after he lost his wife years ago. Donny never told me when his mother had died and why, but those who knew him and his Dad had a lot of sympathy for them. The family was obviously well liked and close-knit. Donny's Dad had gone into a deep depression after his wife had died, and I don't think the flat had been cleaned since then. Donny had grown up missing his Mum and with a Dad who struggled to cope. Most of his income was spent on drugs and drink, so Donny never had a holiday or even a second-hand bike. He grew up too quickly and knew he'd have to make his own way in the world, but he said he didn't feel resentful. He loved his Dad deeply and the fact that he never ended up in care was testimony to the strong bond that held them together despite the odds.

While he was still only a youngster, Donny became involved in crime. He kept away from heroin but took E's at raves and smoked joints, but he always stopped when he'd had enough. His Dad's flat was a useful place to store stolen goods and we often had a smoke round there, but the state of the place really got to me. One day I opened a few boxes of our fake stain remover and washed the walls with the contents. The difference was amazing, but I had to admit that plain water would probably have had almost as much effect!

Kenny's flat was in total contrast to Donny's. I didn't feel moved to do the cleaning there! It was the height of luxury. Kenny often invited Sharky and me round to join him in a champagne breakfast. Kenny lived with Sarah near the seafront in Southend, and kept his money and the drugs there. When I first met Kenny at the start of my home leave from prison, he was in Tottenham living with another woman and her three children. It seems that, aged only twenty-five, he was running two households and maintaining two common-law wives and assorted children. He lived on the edge and pulled in a lot of money. In his flat or in a restaurant Kenny looked very calm, very together, but when he was in his rave club, Beyond Therapy, he was really uptight, almost paranoid. He always had two bouncers near at hand and I discovered he was armed. It was no wonder he was so jumpy. Had there ever been a drugs raid on his club, Kenny would have been in real trouble.

To a certain extent Sharky, Tommy Sellers and I lived double lives too. Much of my time would be spent selling moody goods at car boot sales and breaking into offices at night, but at other times I'd be conning drug dealers out of large sums of money. Sharky was a con man who could act the business man perfectly and was used to dining in top class restaurants. Tommy Sellers was a successful street con man with a lovely wife and son, but he only came to life when he was racing his high performance bikes at 120 mph along the A127.

I was still watching Sharky closely. The idea that he might be conning me had not gone away. Donny and I had moved the remaining stock of stain remover from Tommy Sellers' garage to Donny's flat. There was very little left and Tommy was happy for us to sell it off and pay him his share as we sold it. He trusted us, but when I told Sharky about what we were doing, he became most concerned. He had invested some money in this scam and he not only wanted to make sure he got his full share of the profits but suggested that I should lie to Tommy so that he could take Tommy's share of the profits too. I devised another little test for Sharky. At the end of a week I asked him if I could have the extra money we had made. I didn't really need it, but I wanted to see how he would react. Would he say, 'Yes, that's OK,' would he ask why I needed it, or would he stop me from having it at all? Sharky listened to my request then suggested various ways by which I could earn some extra money. I had found out what I wanted to know. Sharky was not going to agree to me taking a little extra money, nor was he going to ask how much I needed or acknowledge that he still held a substantial amount of my money for me.

I wondered if the others were equally prepared to rip me off and refuse to give me a few pounds unless there was something in it for them. The next time I was due to pay Tommy his share from the sale of the stain remover, I told him I needed some extra cash that week. He agreed immediately that I should take it and the following week he said he'd made his money out of the scam, and I could have his share of the profits on whatever was left of the stock. Other people whom I dealt with had the same attitude when it came to small sums of money. Kenny was the only one I didn't test out. For a start I wasn't doing business with him, but more importantly, he'd already proved himself to be a good and generous friend.

It was June and Anne was keen to book our flight to Jamaica. We went ahead, getting a flight out on 6 July to return on the 20th. I was still a bit tight for money as I'd written off two cars in a matter of weeks. One wasn't my fault. Andrew and Phil had borrowed my Metro to do an office job. They were leaving the scene of the crime, Andrew driving, when they were clocked by the police. Andrew put his foot down, but ended up crashing the car. He and

Phil ran off in different directions. The police caught Andrew, Phil got away and came straight round to Pauline's. He told me what had happened and said I should go to the police station immediately and report my car stolen. I did, but later changed my story saying Pauline had allowed Andrew to borrow it without my knowledge. This meant the charge against Andrew of taking and driving away was dropped. Andrew maintained in court that I had no idea that my car would be used for anything illegal.

I had to buy another car. This time I got a Ford Fiesta. Within days I had managed to reverse it into a concrete post in a car park. The hatchback was so badly damaged I couldn't open it and so the car became useless for street selling and I had to buy a Transit van to replace it. I couldn't claim on the insurance because, although my insurance documents looked genuine, they were as bent as I was.

Although we were going to stay in a cheap place in Montego Bay and our flights were less expensive than when I last went to Jamaica, I still had to rely on Anne paying part of my air fare for me. I knew I needed a decent amount of spending money to take with me and I approached Sharky again. He said he would lift some goods from the Oxford Street shop such as Walkmans and radio cassette players which I could sell in Jamaica, but we both knew that the limit was three such items per person and more couldn't be smuggled through because of the airport's X-ray machines. Sharky's other helpful suggestions were that I asked Tommy to let me have some fake gold chains to sell, and that I got Howard to pay me up front for weed which I'd bring back with me and let him have at cut price.

Up until this point in my life in Southend, I hadn't been involved in selling drugs. With Sharky's previous record I knew the police would be watching him and, as I was a known associate, we'd both be in the frame if there were any big drug deals going down. But the idea of making some money on what I could bring back from Jamaica took hold. I decided not to do any more break-ins so near my holiday because of the risk of getting caught, but instead I'd go round the local dealers and users and see who was prepared to pay up front for some first class dope at a bargain rate. It then occurred to me that I might as well sell them something when I first made contact with them and earn myself some money. Kenny, I was sure, would sell me some stuff at cost price, so I set off for Tottenham to meet him.

Kenny came up with the goods, as I thought he would, and I started selling. Howard at the Oxford Street shop was my first customer. He and his son Nigel lived in Southend and both smoked weed. Howard also gave me £100 to bring back three quarters of an ounce of top grade weed from Jamaica. In England such quality dope would cost at least £150. I made a deal with a dealer and amassed enough money to pay Anne back, cover the accommodation expenses and have some left over for spending. On top of that I also had the items to sell in Jamaica, so when I stood in the queue at passport control at Heathrow I was feeling quite flush and really excited about the holiday.

The woman looked at my passport and back at me. There was something wrong. 'Is anyone travelling with you?' she asked. I indicated Adrian and Anne whose passports she had just checked. Then she told me that the passport I'd given her belonged to a Pauline Smith. 'What!' I exclaimed in disbelief; but it was Pauline's face looking back at me from the photo in the passport. At once I remembered how the night before Pauline had been telling me about the places she'd visited. She thought she'd better make sure her passport hadn't expired so brought it downstairs. She must have left it lying near mine. Obviously in the rush to get to the airport for a 7 am departure I'd picked up the wrong one. I phoned Sharky, who organized a taxi to bring my passport to me at the airport. He took Pauline's passport back to Southend and suddenly my spending money was reduced by the sum of £50. Fortunately the flight was delayed for two hours, so the pressure was eased slightly, though I was still annoyed with myself throughout the journey for making such a stupid mistake.

Our accommodation was pretty grim. The rooms were dirty and the water in the swimming pool was such a funny green colour that no one attempted to swim in it. We booked in for two nights only and made the most of the view which looked out across the bay to the clear blue sea. The next day was spent on a fruitless search for somewhere better to stay, but there was nowhere available for the price we could afford so we decided to move on to Runaway Bay. We piled onto a bus with all our baggage and set off for our destination. I sat with my arm hanging out of the open window and the bus ride sparked so many memories of my last visit that I quite expected to see Bradley suddenly appear with our accommodation sorted – 'no problem, boss!'

The bus pulled up outside the hotel where Sharky, Pauline and I had stayed. I stepped out into the road and there was Bradley! 'Hello, boss,' he said calmly, 'I've been waiting for you.' 'But I didn't tell you I was coming,' I said, nonplussed. 'I saw your arm when you were on the bus,' he laughed. 'I knew it was you.' I introduced Anne and Adrian to Bradley and we went off to the local bar. I told Bradley that we needed somewhere cheap to stay and that we had some goods to sell. As ever, it was no problem for him and he left us for a while then returned with someone I remembered from the time before – the guy who'd provided us with a chalice. He took us to his uncle's place, a short walk from the hotel. It was a two-storey building with five rooms and a kitchen per floor. Each room had a double and a single bed and a bathroom. It would cost us a total of £21 a week if we shared one room, a price which suited us down to the ground. We exchanged one of the Walkmans for an ounce of dope and sat smoking and chilling out on the beach.

After a day of sight-seeing, Bradley arranged for us to see a different site – a field of cannabis plants six feet tall. The field was situated up a steep hill, but it was only the size of a large room. The owner explained that anything bigger would run the risk of being spotted by a police helicopter and if that happened the pilot would land nearby and the crop would be torched. I gave him a radio in exchange for enough weed to last us a week and, as we left the field, Anne picked a big leaf and slipped it into her waist bag. The sun and the amount of dope we were smoking was beginning to tell on us so our next deal was with the chalice man for some cocaine. Although not normally cocaine users, we needed something to pick us up. It cost us a Walkman and caused a fight between the chalice man and Bradley, who thought the former was trying to take his business from him. I calmed Bradley down and showed him the gold chains. We had decided to go from place to place selling the chains if people thought they were real gold, but if Bradley's reaction was anything to go by, Jamaicans knew fake gold when they saw it. His eyes lit up when I drew a chain out of its red pouch, but as soon as he took a closer look he knew it wasn't gold. We realized it was no good trying to pass the chains off as the genuine item, so we gave them to the girls behind the bar and were given a few free drinks. A couple of days later the chains turned black. A combination of salt water and sun had caused some sort of chemical reaction, but the girls weren't bothered and went on wearing them.

We spent most of our second week sun bathing and getting to know the locals. I went night fishing with a couple of blokes and we sat on the rocks dangling fishing lines attached to live bait – soft-shelled crabs – into the ocean. Having no experience or skill, I soon gave up. I rolled the joints while the others fished and when dawn broke we lit a fire, cooked and ate the catch. It was a simple, memorable time. I felt at peace and at one with nature, but the hard realities of my life soon pressed in on me. There were only a few days of our holiday left and I needed to get the weed sorted out that we were going to smuggle back into England. I told Bradley I wanted to go to Three Mile Island for the best sensimillia and I'd need someone with a reliable car to get us there. Bradley's vehicle broke down as soon as you looked at it and the police had already warned him not to take it out on the road. He tried and failed to borrow a car, so he lost the business to the guy who had a car and had refused to lend it to him! We got our top grade weed and visited Trench Town where Bob Marley had lived. The following day was taken up with packing up the dope. Sharky had told us that Anne mustn't carry any drugs back, so it was down to Adrian and me. We made up six sticks and handfuls of balls of the soft weed, then began to pack. Every item had to be sprayed with deodorant or air freshener before it went into a suitcase, to mask the smell of cannabis which had got into the very fibres of our clothes after two weeks of heavy smoking. We couldn't take the chance of our cases being opened at the Heathrow customs, and the contents reeking of cannabis.

The morning of our flight home, Adrian and I swallowed the balls of dope instead of breakfast, but when it came to packing our backsides, he could only manage two sticks so I forced up four. I was still giving our belongings a final spray before we boarded the bus to the airport, when I came across Anne's waist bag and, still inside it, the large leaf she'd picked in the weed field. This worried me because I no longer had time to check all the pockets in her clothing, and she obviously had a memory like a sieve. The journey to Montego Bay airport didn't take very long, but I was in a lot of pain when we arrived, and was bitterly regretting my decision to try and conceal four rather than three sticks of dope. We passed through customs and boarded the plane with no delays. As soon as I could, I went into the toilet and removed the troublesome stick. I had a comfortable flight back and, before we landed, I returned to the toilet and reinserted the fourth stick. I was conscious of the damage I could do to myself and of the risk of arrest if I couldn't withstand the ensuing pain, but I found that the other sticks had settled and the extra stick didn't hurt.

The three of us sat apart on the plane, so when we landed I went through customs on my own and Anne and Adrian came through later as a couple. I walked along the 'Nothing to Declare' channel and arrived at passport control where a number of customs officers were waiting. One of them checked my passport and asked if I was travelling alone. I said I was with a couple but explained that we'd not been sitting together. The officer asked me to wait for them there, so we could go through customs together. When I saw Anne and Adrian I gave them a friendly wave to warn them not to deny that we were travelling together. They told the customs officers the same as I had, and we were then escorted to a place with a long bench on which we had to place our bags. We stood beside them while one of the officers took our passports and disappeared to an office out of our sight. Anne was getting very nervous and I did my best to reassure her, although I was feeling really edgy myself. But luck was with us. The officer came back, returned our passports then let us through, without even opening a single bag.

Sharky was waiting for us and we stacked our bags into the cavernous boot of his Saab 900 and set off for Southend. I told him about our brush with customs and he checked the traffic behind us, speeding up for a few minutes then slowing down to see if we were being tailed. Customs have the power to follow you and stop you outside the airport limits, but there was no sign of anything amiss so he drove home at a steady 60 mph. We dropped Adrian off and I delivered the weed to those who'd paid me for it up front. We settled down at Pauline's to enjoy some of the remaining dope. When Pauline and Sharky had gone to bed Anne produced a ball that we'd wrapped up for swallowing. She'd smuggled it through just to experience the buzz, but she begged me not to tell her Mum. At first I was a bit annoyed with her, but it didn't last. I just pointed out that if I'd known she was going to bring dope through, I'd have loaded her up with the stuff!

After two weeks, which floated by in a haze of dope smoking, I got back to street selling and burglary, but it all went wrong when I started working with Donny and a bloke called Alan. Alan was an opportunist thief, willing to try anything regardless of the risk. We were driving around in my Transit van when he asked me to pull over. He'd seen a brewery lorry parked round the back of an off-licence. In no time at all he had us helping him offload packs of cans of beer into the van. Passers-by looked but said nothing. After a few minutes I jumped back into the van, keen to get away, but Alan wanted to go and get just one more pack, then just another one. While we hung around for Alan, Donny noticed a man making a note of the Transit's registration number. We took the beer to a mate of Alan's who had converted the shed in his back garden into a bar and sold drinks after the pubs shut. We sold it all to him except for one pack each. I knew I had no option but to dump the Transit. I drove to a car park, wiped all the finger prints and broke the ignition so it could be started without a key, then reported it stolen.

Two days later I borrowed Adrian's car. Sarah, Kenny's common-law wife in Southend, had just had a baby girl and I drove round to her flat with Donny to give Sarah a card and a present. We took a look at the little one in the bedroom, then went to the lounge and smoked a couple of joints before leaving. I had taken a strong sleeping pill earlier and this, plus the dope, had a disastrous affect on my concentration. Driving along Southend's seafront, I missed the turning for Pauline's place and decided to go back around the roundabout. I slewed the car round then drove straight into a concrete post, one of a line along the roadside put there to prevent vehicles mounting the pavement. I was so out of it that I didn't even brake.

Donny wasn't wearing a seat belt. He was thrown forward and his head hit the windscreen, with such force that the screen shattered. I was unhurt. I opened the car door and got out. As I went to go round to the passenger door a guy came racing up to me and punched me in the face. 'That's my cousin,' he snarled and hit me again. Donny levered himself out of the car. 'Leave it, he's all right,' he muttered. 'He never even slowed down!' retorted his cousin angrily. 'He's a nutter!' Somehow, despite the pain he was in, Donny managed to calm him down and he walked off swearing that he had better be OK or he'd come looking for me.

As he left, the police arrived. They radioed for an ambulance and asked me the sort of questions I didn't want to answer: 'Are you the owner of this vehicle?' 'Were you driving?' 'You look a bit drunk, are you on any medication?' The ambulance arrived, and the police accompanied Donny and me to the hospital. After we had been checked out and told we could leave, the police charged me with driving without due care and attention, and gave me a ticket to produce the car's documents at a police station in the next five days.

Adrian was not a happy man. I couldn't pay him then and there for the damage I'd done, but I promised I would get the money together. Adrian didn't believe me and he stopped coming round after the accident. I was charged with failing to produce the vehicle's documents at a police station, but it didn't bother me. I carried on shifting moody goods on the streets using Tommy Sellers' car to transport the stock.

One Saturday, a few weeks after the crash, I arrived back at Pauline's at the end of a day's selling, to be met at the door by Phil. He looked pale and shocked. 'Kenny's dead,' he said, staring at me as if he couldn't believe what he was saying. 'What? How?' was the only response I was capable of making. I pushed past Phil and went into the front room, where Pauline and Sharky were sitting with stunned expressions on their faces. Between them they told me all they knew. In the early hours of the morning, Kenny was in a car with a couple of mates returning from a club. He passed out and started to turn blue. Kenny was used to taking a number of different drugs, so the fact that he had had acid, E's, some pills to bring him back down and had smoked some puff that night was nothing out of the ordinary for him. But this time his mates could see that there was something seriously wrong. They tried to bring him round but failed, so they drove as fast as they could to the nearest hospital. It was too late. Kenny was dead on arrival.

I'd scarcely taken this in when Valerie, Pauline's eldest daughter, arrived with Sarah and the baby. I wanted to express my sympathy to Sarah but I just couldn't find the right words. Sharky was still in shock. He looked straight ahead and kept muttering, 'That's permanent.' Sarah couldn't stop crying. She was finding it nearly impossible to come to terms with the fact that her twenty-five-year-old partner, father of her six-week-old baby, was dead. I kept thinking that I was having a bad dream and would wake up soon, or that Kenny would walk through the door and we'd find out that a mistake had been made. Someone else had died, not him.

By the end of that long evening, we had come to accept that Kenny was dead and we did all we could to support Sarah over the next few days. Kenny's parents organized the funeral. They invited everyone who had known their son. There was a big turnout, which included a lot of people I'd never seen before. The police were also conspicuous by their presence – making note of many of the registration numbers of the cars parked at the crematorium. Kenny's father spoke at the funeral. He mentioned the club and said that Kenny was 'Beyond Therapy' now. The coffin slid away and the curtains closed behind it. I'd written a goodbye message on the card to go with my wreath. It went like this:

> 'Twenty-five seems so young to die
> We look around and say why, oh why
> Although he was no more
> Than just a big kid
> Of life he took a good lick.
> R.I.P. Kenny.'

After the service we went on to a hall where the wake was held. There was a generous supply of food and drink, but as time went on I felt an increasing sense of tension about the gathering. Among the mourners was Gabby. Her boyfriend had a reputation in Southend and was known as Big Bob. He was in prison, so Gabby had come on her own. She was a moaner with a loud, penetrating voice and the drink both loosened her tongue and increased the volume. People had quietened her down a couple of times, but it didn't last. Irritated by her voice and embarrassed by her behaviour, I marched over to her and said, 'Why don't you do everyone a favour and go home? No one wants you here anyway.' I'd gone too far. 'What do you mean? Who doesn't want me here?' she screamed in my face.

Right on cue, two of Big Bob's mates came over. Sharky and Thumper, one of Kenny's bouncers, tried to calm things down. Thumper drew me to one side. 'Listen Mick, just get back there and apologize to her,' he urged me. Reluctantly, I accompanied him back to where Gabby was standing with a small group of supporters. I told her I was out of order and that I'd lied when I said that people didn't want her to be at the wake. Big Bob's friends told me to go and sober up. Sharky and Thumper got me out of the hall smartish and walked me up and down the road until I'd cooled down. We returned to the wake and there was no more trouble. Later we took a taxi home, leaving Sharky's Saab outside the hall. We were all too drunk to drive.

The next morning I was coping with my hangover in my usual fashion – drinking black coffee and smoking a joint – when Sharky came into the room. He laid into me immediately. 'Do you realize how much trouble you nearly caused last night?' He didn't wait for an answer. 'I don't need to be having to explain you to these sort of people,' he continued, getting more incensed. When I still didn't respond he put his face close to mine and snarled, 'You're lucky they didn't take lumps out of you.' He went on and on, until it developed into a shouting match. At last he stormed out of the room and went back upstairs. I started to drink the rest of my coffee and then I saw the keys to the Saab lying on the table. I pictured Devon and the peace and quiet I'd known there and thought, 'Why not?' I picked up the keys, slipped them into my pocket and went to my bedroom to put on my shoes and coat and collect my stash of weed, then I left the house. I walked to the top of the road and phoned for a taxi from a public telephone box.

The taxi dropped me at the hall. I unlocked the Saab, turned the key in the ignition and headed out of Southend.

I'd travelled several miles down the motorway before I thought about whether what I was doing was right or wrong. Until then I was only concerned about my hangover and my overwhelming need for tranquillity. It took only seconds for me to decide that if I never went back to Southend, all Sharky had lost was a car, and between us we had conned people out of a lot more money than he had spent on the Saab.

I arrived at John and Lyn's front door, hoping they'd be there and not in Basingstoke. Lyn opened the door and was surprised and delighted to see me. I told her and John about Kenny and once we'd caught up with the rest of the news, John suggested we went and bought some beers. When he saw the Saab he wanted to drive it! I didn't mind. I'd had enough of driving for that day, especially as I'd been suffering from a hangover for much of the journey.

As we drove through the country lanes, John noticed a police car in the rear view mirror. He accelerated away, but once we reached a straight stretch of road, we saw that the police car wasn't far behind, so it was either tailing us or in a hurry to get somewhere else. John asked me if he should find out whether we were being followed or not. 'Yeah, go on then,' I said casually and he put his foot down. The Saab leapt forward, but the police car kept pace with us. John said we were coming up to an old castle. He'd drive round it and once we were out of sight he could walk away from the car as if it was nothing to do with him.

He drove like mad and managed to put some distance between us and the police. John was out of the car and walking down a grassy slope when the police car came into view. The driver positioned the car across the gateway so it blocked the drive to the castle grounds. I walked down the driveway towards the police. Another police car pulled up as an officer approached me and asked if I had just driven into the grounds. 'Yes,' I answered innocently. 'Why?' 'What car were you driving?' he persisted, not impressed by my artless response. There were only two cars parked by the castle wall. 'The Saab,' I replied. 'In that case,' he continued, 'I'm arresting you for stealing a car.'

I was genuinely taken aback, and went to great lengths to explain how I'd had a row with a mate, who probably didn't realize I'd borrowed his motor. The officer wasn't interested. His colleagues had gone round the back of the castle by now and he just wanted to know who had been in the car with me. I insisted that I was the only occupant, but he swore he'd seen someone else. I stuck to my story. The policemen from the second car reappeared. They had John. I was handcuffed and then we were taken in separate cars to the police station. We were left on a bench together outside a charge room and were careful to ignore one another. My inquisitor came up to me and, indicating John, said, 'This is the one who was in the car with you isn't it? He was driving.' I denied it and told him he didn't know what he was talking about. I was searched and I told the story about Kenny and Sharky all over again to the police officer in the charge room. I even gave him Sharky's phone number so he could check it out, but meanwhile I was locked in a cell.

Ten minutes later, they were back wanting to know why there were stacks of gold chains in the boot of the car! I explained that they were cheap rolled gold necklaces that my friend sold on the market. When they came back the next time it was to tell me that Sharky had confirmed my story and wanted to speak to me. I was glad Sharky had come up trumps, but I wondered what he was going to say to me when it was me and not the Old Bill on the phone. It was short and to the point. The trouble between us would be forgotten, but I must drive straight back with the car because he needed it. The police released me without charge and returned the car to me. They charged John with driving offences, then let him go. He had admitted that he was in the car, but when his case went to court, he was going to plead not guilty and swear that he was only a passenger.

I took John back home, then headed off for Southend. The journey was incident free even though I thought I might be stopped by the police because the car had been reported stolen. Sharky was pleased to have the Saab back and we enjoyed a smoke together. He and Pauline told me that they really thought the car had been stolen and that's why they'd reported it to the police, but during the conversation Pauline acknowledged that she knew I had friends in Devon. I reckoned they must have sussed that I had taken the car as soon as they discovered the keys had gone, and yet again I questioned how far I could trust Sharky.

John's case came up before the magistrates in Barnstaple not long after I'd returned from Jamaica. The sun tan hadn't even started to fade. I had another car on the road, and I drove down to Devon the night before the court hearing. John and I rehearsed what we were going to say and he suggested that I told the magistrates that I'd flown back specially from Jamaica to attend the court, in the hope that I could claim my return air fare if he was found not guilty.

I proved once again how well I could keep a straight face when talking a load of rubbish. Having taken an oath to tell the truth, the whole truth and nothing but the truth, I swore that John had been the passenger in the Saab and I had been the driver. In response to the police allegation that the car had been driven without due care and attention to other road users, I insisted that I was used to high performance cars and that, although I had been driving at speed, I was fully in control of the vehicle. When the prosecution put it to me that the police had had a clear view of the driver, I refuted that claim by pointing out that the Saab was travelling at between 60 and 70 mph, had high backed seats and was travelling along a narrow road lined with high hedges. My interrogation ended with the question: 'Is it true to say that you cut short your holiday in Jamaica in order to give evidence in this court today?' I replied that that was indeed true and stood down. John was found not guilty, and as we left the court room his solicitor told me that if I could give him proof of the date I flew back, he could claim back the cost of my air fare. Since I had no such proof, I had reluctantly to forgo the pleasure of being paid handsomely for lying my head off.

After Kenny's funeral, Sharky and Pauline's relationship started to fall apart. Pauline had a massive row with Sharky. She accused him of being cold and heartless, of not even shedding a tear over the death of his friend. It cast doubts on how much he felt for her. Sharky's reaction was to start looking for somewhere else to live. The person I really felt sorry for was Sarah. I often saw her walking the baby in the park, her face twisted with grief and loneliness. I was on my own with Pauline one day, talking about Kenny, and she saw the tears in my eyes. Our conversation moved on to considering what happened when someone died. I said I believed in Heaven and Hell and was certain that I was going to Hell. At least, I told Pauline, I would know plenty of people there and, as for being judged, I'd done what I'd done and nothing could change it, so I'd get what was coming to me. Pauline said Sharky had read lots of books about the after-life and religion and was convinced that when you died that was the end of the story. You lived this life and that was it, so you might as well make the most of it while you were here.

Pauline had different ideas. She thought there must be more, and she was finding out about meditation and how to get on a higher spiritual plane. We came back to the present situation with her and Sharky, and she asked me if I would take her away to Devon for a few days. Sharky thought it would be good for everyone too and said we could have the Saab and he'd use Pauline's Ford Sierra while we were away. As it was the school holidays, we had to take Pauline's youngest daughter, Claire, with us. I phoned John and Lyn and asked them to book us into a guest house near them, but they insisted that we stayed with them. Claire was so excited she wanted to leave at once, but I had to help at the Wembley market that weekend, so we set off on the Monday.

Pauline and I shared the driving and had a trouble free journey. John and Lyn made us very welcome and Hazel and Claire got on like a house on fire. We took the girls to some lovely beaches and chilled out. I did try selling some stain remover with John at his local markets but it was a waste of time. Every punter wanted to look inside the box, see the instructions and ask awkward questions, so we gave up. On the Friday we drove to a restaurant in a small village. It was very hilly but the view was amazing. Unfortunately, on the way back, the car started to play up. We checked under the bonnet but could find nothing wrong. It finally conked out at the bottom of a hill and we had to leave it there and arrange for a local garage to go out and tow it back. We phoned Sharky before we left Devon to tell him about the car and the three of us caught a train back to Southend.

Two days after our return, Sharky announced that he was moving out. He said he was going to keep Pauline's Sierra as he reckoned we'd made arrangements with John to sell the Saab in Devon: that was, he added, if we hadn't already sold it and spent the money. Sharky moved in with another woman who had a house on the outskirts of Southend. I stayed with Pauline. She was furiously angry and wanted to go to the police about her car. I persuaded her to wait until I'd had a chance to talk to Sharky. I met up with him a few days later, but nothing I said made any difference. With barely veiled contempt, he told me that he had had the hire purchase agreement on the Sierra changed to his name so Pauline could run to the police as many times as she liked, it would get her nowhere. He refused to believe that we hadn't planned to con him out of his Saab while we were in Devon, and warned me that if I wanted to start doing things my way, he would make sure I got no more work from Tommy Sellers and the Oxford Street shop.

That night Pauline and I talked long and hard. I now knew that Sharky was the sort of man who always wanted to be in control, and who was prepared to use people until they had served his purpose. Then he'd cast them aside like dirty rags. We had two choices, in my opinion. We could let things be and just make sure the hire purchase company knew Sharky had the car, so if John got the Saab sorted out Pauline would have a car that was paid for, and I would continue working with Sharky and would start paying Pauline rent. The alternative was to cut off Sharky's means of earning money before he brought mine to an end. I'd felt angry with Sharky following our meeting, but that had faded and had been replaced by the hollow feeling of being let down, made a fool of. I had put all my trust, my hopes and dreams in this guy and he'd thrown it back in my face, just because of a misunderstanding over a car. Or maybe he thought I was having an affair with Pauline, which couldn't have been further from the truth. I explained to Pauline that I had a plan to get our revenge on Sharky, but if I put it into action I would have to leave Southend. We agreed to go for it.

Early the next morning I set off to catch Howard before he left for the Oxford Street shop. As I walked along the seafront to Howard's flat I thought about what I would do if I were Sharky. I remembered times when I'd done burglaries and had found the money while my mates were in another part of the building. When we'd got away from the house or office I would always split the cash fifty-fifty, and that was when there was only a couple of hundred to be had at the very best. Sharky and I had taken thousands of pounds from moody drug deals and had he shared it fairly with me, I should have had at least fifteen grand. Instead I had nothing, not even a car of my own. He had conned me, like he conned everyone else, and it was a bitter pill to swallow.

I rang the bell and put my face in clear view of the security camera, so Howard could see who was calling. Through the intercom I told him I needed to talk to him and he pushed the button to release the door catch. Normally I only called on Howard when I had a message or a package from Sharky, so I felt a bit awkward and ill at ease. Howard noticed and told me to sit down while his son Nigel fixed me a cup of coffee. I made myself comfortable in an armchair and Howard returned from the kitchen and rolled us a couple of joints. I started to tell him about the goods Sharky was taking out of the back door of the shop and selling on the streets and at car boot sales. He was fiddling the shop accounts too, I continued, which was why he wouldn't take any time off from the shop in case he was found out.

Nigel had brought the coffee in, and when he heard this, he ran into his bedroom and came back with a baseball bat. He was all for using Sharky's head as the ball, but Howard calmed him down and said it would be sorted out with the London firm. I didn't know who they were, but I did know that they owned the shop and Howard was answerable to them for the profits it made. He asked me a hundred and one questions and I answered as many as I could, such as where he could find Sharky's lock-up, how many items were stolen per delivery, what happened to the money taken from the street sales and finally the question I knew he would ask: 'Mick, you know this could have serious consequences?' I had to explain why I was dropping Sharky in it and I told Howard I was skint because Sharky had, in effect, stolen my money from me, and that now I wanted the satisfaction of knowing that he wouldn't have any more money coming in either.

Howard asked me to show him the garage in Wickford. I agreed and he gave me the keys to a Datsun Nigel was using as a runaround. He followed me and when we arrived I pushed up the garage door to show him the stack of radio cassettes, Walkmans, Nintendos and other items supposedly destined for the shop. Howard surveyed the contents of the garage, grim-faced, then told me to lock up and give him the key. 'How long's he been doing this, Mick?' he asked as he turned the key in the lock. 'More or less since the shop started,' I replied. 'And Sharky has a few grand of yours that you know of?' he went on. 'Yeah,' I said resignedly. Howard took the

Datsun's log book out of his pocket and gave it to me. 'You can keep the car,' he said, then turned on his heel and walked over to his motor. We went our separate ways.

I headed back to Southend, pleased to have my own set of wheels again, and decided to go and tell Pauline about my meeting with Howard. She heard me out, then asked me what was likely to happen to Sharky. I said I thought he would probably be able to talk his way out of trouble, but if not he might end up inside a concrete pillar supporting a flyover somewhere. I reckoned we'd know the score that night. I was sure that Sharky would be in touch, and I warned Pauline not to listen to anything he told her but to tell him she was only interested in her car.

I left Pauline's and went to see Donny. I told him I wanted to do a couple of jobs because I needed some ready money, and said I had a car so we could drive round and look out for some likely places. We picked out an office. It was at the top of a three-storey building and he said he'd fancied it before, the only drawback being that it was situated by a busy road. Since there was a side entrance, we decided we'd take our chances when the time was right. I dropped Donny off at his flat and returned to Pauline's to find out if she'd heard anything from Sharky. I thought he might have been kicked out of the shop with a beating and a warning not to come back, but Pauline had heard nothing.

Two hours later Sharky phoned. 'What have you been saying to Howard, Mick?' he asked. There was a note of defeat in his voice, but it was impossible to tell whether it was genuine or not. 'You know what I've told him,' I replied curtly. Sharky said he wanted to see me and Pauline, so I arranged to meet him at Southend bus station in half an hour. She thought it was a strange place to meet, but I explained that he might bring someone else with him, intending to break our legs to teach us a lesson, so being in a public place would give us some protection. Again I reminded Pauline not to let Sharky talk her round. We took the bus to the rendezvous.

He was waiting for us and wanted us to get in the car, but I refused and told him to park up and join us for a walk. Sharky didn't argue. He was obviously in a conciliatory mood and was hoping to sort things out so that he lost nothing. I immediately set him straight. My only concern was to get my hands on my half of the cash. At first Sharky tried to convince me that the money was tied up in the shop and that he couldn't get it released for the time being. I pointed out to him that the money always seemed to be tied up apart for the odd fifty pounds. Then he took a different approach, and offered to get me a van. I told him it was too late. He couldn't get round me. I'd told Howard everything.

Sharky fell silent. We walked around a patch of grass. Pauline watched us from a bench a few metres away. He stopped suddenly and looked at me despairingly. 'Do you realize what you've done?' he asked. 'We had ten grand in that shop. We've lost that and they want me to come up with another ten grand by Monday or they'll take lumps out of me. I'm totally skint now.' 'So am I,' I replied grimly, 'like on day one of coming out of prison.'

He gave up on me for a while and decided to talk to Pauline on her own. First he quizzed me on how much she knew. I said I'd told her very little about what had gone on at the shop. After a brief chat with her, he persuaded us to go for a meal with him. As soon as we'd ordered he started on the tack I knew he would eventually take. Having stressed how much money was at stake, he said he was confident it could all be sorted out to our advantage. All I had to do was to go and see Howard and tell him that, although there was a minor fiddle going on, I'd exaggerated it out of all proportion, because I was upset since I hadn't made as much money from investing in the shop as I'd expected. Sharky said he'd back me up and that the whole business would blow over. I cut him short there. Go down that road, and I'd be the one Howard and company would do over.

Sharky tried one last throw of the dice. He said he had a mumble coming up that was worth eighty grand, but he needed to be in the shop to pull it off. I was expecting something like this, but I let him go on and on, until hours later he finally realized that nothing he said would make any difference. He asked Pauline if he could keep her car for a bit longer so he could drive around and get some money together to pay the guys from the shop. I thought she should have demanded the return of her car then and there, but that was up to her. As far as I was concerned it was time to move on. I was going to do a couple of jobs and then hot foot it to Devon.

Eight

Back Inside

I sat in Donny's flat at one o'clock in the morning, watching the minutes tick by. We were going to do the office job in an hour or so, when there wouldn't be much traffic about. I had decided to leave for Devon once we'd done the job, and I told him that if he wanted to sell the rest of the stain remover, we could do a deal with the cash we'd get from the office safe. He was happy with that arrangement and, when the time came, we picked up our gloves, a bunch of assorted keys, a crowbar and a heavy hammer. I checked my pockets to make sure there was nothing to identify me with the scene of the crime, and as a safeguard in case we were stopped by the police on the way to the job. If that happened, I could give a false name and address and still do the job later.

We got into the Datsun and drove to Alan's house. He was the one who'd seen the safe, so we had to include him. With Alan on board, we went straight to the office block and parked in a side road. The coast was clear, so Alan put the crowbar to good effect on the outer doors. We climbed the stairs to the third floor. I tried out some of my keys on the office door, and soon found one which fitted the lock. By sliding it quickly backwards and forwards, I managed to knock down all the tumblers in the lock and triumphantly swung open the door. Alan went over to a picture hanging on the office wall. He lifted it clear, revealing the small wall safe.

Donny was keeping watch from the window at the front of the office. It looked out over the main road. I helped Alan. I gave the wall on one side of the safe a couple of whacks with the hammer and Alan lifted the plaster off with the crowbar. This was the most risky part of the job. The noise of every hammer blow made me cringe. It was such a giveaway, but it was the quickest way we knew to get our hands on the safe. The brickwork was soon exposed. I started work on the other side of the safe, but Donny told me to stop. We fell silent. Donny ducked down out of sight of the window.

We waited until Donny indicated that it was all clear outside, then we began again. Leaving Alan to prise the bricks away from each side of the safe, Donny and I checked the offices on the floor below. We looked behind pictures for wall safes and searched cupboards and drawers for cash boxes, but we found nothing so we went back to see how Alan was getting on. He had removed the bricks surrounding the steel bars which held the safe in the wall. Usually it took only a few minutes to pull the safe out, but he was struggling. Even with two of us pulling on the safe, it wouldn't budge. Alan decided to continue demolishing the wall around the safe, until we could reach the bar at the back and then we could try and lever it from the wall. We set to work with a will and were removing the inner breeze blocks, when we saw a beam of light shining through the window and onto the ceiling.

We crouched down, and Alan and I crept to the other side of the building. I peeked out of the window and my heart sank when I saw two police officers looking across from the other side of the road. We made our way back and from another window saw a police car pulling up outside our office block. We had two choices. We could go down and hand ourselves over to the Old Bill or we could try and find somewhere to hide. It didn't take long for us to acknowledge that even if the police found it difficult to locate us, their dogs would soon sniff us out. 'Come on, Alan, we might as well go,' I said resignedly. We made our way down to the next floor. We looked in all the offices and called out to Donny to tell him we were giving ourselves up, but there was no sign of him anywhere. We assumed he was going to take his chance and hide. If Alan and I gave ourselves up it could work in his favour. The police would probably take a quick look round then drive us back to the station without bothering to call out a dog unit.

Alan and I reached the glass entrance door to the office block. There were two policemen outside – one was on his radio and the other was trying to force the door open. When we'd used the crowbar we hadn't broken the lock so once inside we'd been able to secure the door. I released the catches and, as we went out, one of the policemen grabbed my sleeve. 'What are you doing in there?' he demanded aggressively. 'I work there,' I replied, keeping a straight face. 'What, at this time of night?' he sneered. 'What do you do?' 'Safe removing,' I said with a grin. At times like these I liked to cheer myself up by giving stupid answers to stupid questions. They handcuffed me and one of them sat beside me in the back of the police car. Alan was put in another vehicle and moments later the dog unit arrived. It looked as though the game was up for Donny as well as us.

When I was questioned at the police station I didn't bother to deny anything. We'd been caught red-handed, so I freely admitted that the large bunch of keys I carried were to help me gain entrance illegally to homes and offices, and that the Datsun parked outside the offices was my car. At the end of the interview I was told I'd be charged with breaking and entering, criminal damage and going equipped. I was given five days in which to produce the documents for the car, which was impounded until I complied. My fingerprints were taken for the umpteenth time in my criminal career, and the following morning I was charged and released on police bail. Alan and Donny were given the same treatment and once we were free we went our separate ways.

My priority was to sort out some insurance for the car. For fifty pounds the bent insurance man provided me with a back-dated cover note for the Datsun and I was able to get my car back. My money situation was pretty bleak and I decided to catch up with Donny and see if he wanted to go out with me, selling some of the remaining stain remover. First I drove to Pauline's to let her know what was happening. She thought I might have been locked up, because the police had been round and had gone through my belongings. I explained the situation and moved on to Donny's flat.

He had someone with him, Peter, a guy I'd seen a couple of times before. We chatted about the events of the previous night, then Peter asked if we would be interested in something he had lined up. I said I was interested in anything which would guarantee me some cash. Peter warned us that the place was belled up, but if we could do the job, he had a buyer for all the stuff we could steal. This was good news and he had my undivided attention.

Peter explained that his uncle was the cash buyer and the place he was looking to do over was a golf club. Although there was a bar there, it had recently been broken into and since then a separate alarm system had been installed, so we decided to concentrate on the shop. Two days later we drove to the golf club at one in the morning. The area surrounding it was quite flat so we would be able to see anyone coming from some distance away. All was quiet as we parked in a lane just behind some houses across the road from the golf club. A hedge ran along one side of the lane, affording us good cover, and there was a subway under the road. We walked through the subway and climbed the fence into the club grounds, then made straight for the golf shop. Peter carried a short scaffold pole which he used to knock the alarm off the wall. The alarm started ringing, but once Peter had buried it in some sand there was silence. We retreated to the other side of the road and waited for the police to turn up.

It didn't take them long. Two cars arrived and the officers spent ten to fifteen minutes looking around before they got back into their cars and drove off apparently satisfied that nothing untoward was going on. We sat tight for another twenty minutes in case they came back. 'Do you reckon that's long enough?' I asked Peter. 'Tell you what – if you go to the car and fetch the tools, me and Donny will wait here and keep an eye on the building,' he replied. I headed off to the car and collected the long screwdriver, crowbar and black bin bags which Peter had stowed in the boot. He'd been thinking about doing this job for some time and knew exactly what tools he'd need. When I returned he said there'd been no sign of the police, so we decided to go for it.

The bottom half of the shop door was wooden, the top half glass covered with a wire frame. There were two locks on the door so it was easier to rip off the wire covering and smash the glass. Peter and I climbed through carefully. He handed the golf clubs to me and I passed them out to Donny. Once we'd cleared all the clubs we started filling the bags with smaller items. Suddenly Donny hissed, 'On top!' Peter and I dived for cover. I hid under the counter and as I lay there I heard a car pull up outside. I was hoping for the best, but I knew I didn't stand a chance. I heard the police climb in and the crunch of broken glass under their feet, then I was nose to nose with an Alsatian. As I clambered out through the door I saw Donny stepping up into a police van. Behind me the dog handler rooted Peter out of his hiding place. It seemed as if we and the police had played a waiting game – and we'd lost.

The following day, we appeared before the magistrates and applied for bail. It was refused and we were remanded in custody for seven days. It came as no surprise and we settled down in Cheltenham prison for the week. While we were there I was interviewed by a probation officer. She asked me if I wanted her to try and get me into a bail hostel when I made my next court appearance. I was all for it, but I didn't think the court would agree because of my record. On one occasion I had been given three years on probation on condition that I stayed in a hostel. On day eight I received my giro, went into town, stole a car and never returned. After the police caught up with me I was given a second term of borstal training instead and I had broken every probation order I'd ever been given, so she was wasting her time. She looked through the paperwork in silence, then indicated a good probation report from when I was given community work in Devon. 'Yeah,' I laughed, 'but look what they gave me. Two hundred hours for shoplifting.' The probation officer refused to be put off. Since I didn't have a home to call my own there was a chance that the hostel would arrange a flat or bedsit for me at the end of the order. Now she was talking. I told her I was keen to move away from Southend and make a fresh start. In court the following week, the probation officer made a good case for me to go into a hostel, and to my delight I was given bail as long as I lived in the bail hostel. I agreed the terms. Donny and Peter got bail too. Donny was particularly lucky as he was already on police bail for the safe job.

By the time I arrived at the hostel in Stratford I had convinced myself that everything was going to work out well. If I behaved myself and was given a good report, I might be given twelve months probation to be served while staying at the hostel. Best of all, this would get me out of Southend and provide me with a place of my own. The police had impounded the Datsun, so I had to go from Basildon magistrates' court to Southend, pick up some clothes and other personal belongings, then take a train to Stratford and arrive at the hostel by seven at the latest.

I made it in time, and soon discovered that the hostel was an easy-going place with staff you could talk to. I made friends with a bloke called Gavin Cooper who liked a puff. Gavin, another guy called Ernie and I went round the town together most days and enjoyed a couple of pints in the evening. The hostel had a 10 pm curfew, so we kept an eye on the time. It didn't bother us too much as we had very little money to spend. Once back at the hostel we would go to one of our rooms for a smoke.

After my first two weeks at the hostel, I asked the staff if I could have my car there. They had no objections, but said I'd have to find somewhere to park it. The police were willing to return the car to me, but I had to come up with a good story to explain why the only insurance document I could show them was an old cover note. Amazingly they believed me when I said I'd been lodging with a mate who'd split up with his common-law wife. In a fit of revenge she'd destroyed all his belongings, mistakenly including some of mine. The insurance policy had been in amongst it all, and I had informed the insurance company and requested a replacement policy. Gavin and I drove back to Stratford in high spirits. It was always gratifying to get one over on the Old Bill.

Across the road from the hostel was a garage where we bought our fags when the shops were shut. The staff turned a blind eye to our slipping over the road for cigarettes after curfew. The guy who worked there was happy for me to park the car in a corner of the forecourt and I was able to see it from the window of my room.

Gavin was from Dagenham so we would often drive there for a drink. It made a welcome change from the pubs near the hostel. Ernie usually came along too. He was a good laugh and so well-built that nobody gave us any grief. While we were out and about, we took the opportunity to do the odd job to provide us with cash for petrol and dope. Usually it involved nicking a stereo out of a car or stealing a video recorder from a house. We could sell such items easily with no questions asked.

When we couldn't find any easy pickings, money quickly became a major concern. We had nothing in reserve for the lean times and on one occasion it looked as though we were going to have to go without and wait for the next giro. We arrived back at the hostel in the afternoon. There was hardly anyone else in. As we walked past one bloke's room Ernie nudged me and said, 'He's got a stereo in there.' I thought for a moment. 'No, leave it. He's all right.' I replied. But he had already stopped outside the door. With one mighty kick he broke the lock and the door swung open. He walked in and unplugged the stereo. 'What the hell are you doing?' I asked angrily. 'The guy's OK. Let's just go and do a house any house, if you want money that bad.' Ernie didn't reply. He just spun round on his heels and punched me full on the jaw.

The punch broke my jaw, and knocked me out for a couple of minutes. When I came round a member of staff was kneeling beside me. He said he'd seen Ernie running down the stairs and asked me what had happened. Why was I in someone else's room that had obviously been broken into? How come he'd found me lying unconscious on the floor? I tried to speak, but a sharp pain in my jaw stopped me. I realized I was quite badly hurt. Two more staff members entered the room. One said he was going to phone for the police and an ambulance. They were going to tell the police to pick up Ernie, as they believed he was responsible for the break-in and my smashed jaw. Since they'd sussed what had gone on, I didn't feel too bad about telling them that Ernie was indeed the culprit.

The doctors wired my jaw together, and for the next few weeks I had all my food in liquid form and drank it through a straw. Ernie kept well clear of the hostel and most of the guys there showed me a lot of sympathy. A few of them were keen to do Ernie for stealing from someone who was in the same boat as him. I saw him only once after the incident. It was late at night and he climbed the drainpipe and tapped on my window. I wondered what was going on as I crossed the room to draw back the curtains. When I saw it was Ernie I pushed up the window and let him in. I must admit that I did think about pushing him off the window sill, but I resisted the temptation. I told him the police were looking for him, but he said he'd wanted to come back to apologize to me. 'I was out of order there. See ya later,' and he was gone.

Things were looking up. Gavin went to court and was given an order of condition of residence, so he was installed in a flat at the back of the hostel. I enjoyed going round there for a smoke and, as he had a cooker, we often had a meal together. We made friends with a new resident of the hostel, Geoff Hunter, and the three of us shared our giros so we could have a drink together every few days.

It was my turn to go to court. I had a good report from the bail hostel, I hadn't got into trouble with the police and the probation officer even told the court that I had suffered a broken jaw when I'd tried to stop another resident from breaking into someone's room. It was looking good until the case for the prosecution was made. Since there was a big age gap between me and Donny and Peter, it was suggested that I had led them into a life of crime, teaching them to break into different buildings. With the golf club burglary following so soon after the safe job, suddenly my prospects didn't seem so bright. The magistrate decided to take a serious view of my past conduct and, to my horror, sentenced me to nine months in prison.

Throughout my time in Chelmsford prison I kept in touch with Gavin and Geoff . They sold my car for me, wrote to me and visited, bringing in some puff as requested. By the time I was due to be discharged, Gavin was renting a flat in Woolwich overlooking the Woolwich ferry, and Geoff had been given condition of residence at the hostel. Gavin said I could move in with him when I was released, and I took him up on his offer. All my property from Southend was still in the hostel, but it only took a couple of trips to pick it up and take it to Woolwich. Gavin came with me each time and we went for a pint with Geoff. The staff were pleased to see us, but most of the residents we knew had moved on.

Gavin's flat was sparsely furnished. I was going to sleep on a bed settee in his front room while he slept on a mattress in his bedroom. I needed to earn some money, but I didn't fancy getting a job. My criminal record and the fact that I hadn't had a proper job for years meant that I'd find it difficult to get employment on a building site or in a factory. I was used to selling, though, and when I noticed that there was only one bloke in Woolwich selling *The Big Issue* I thought I'd give it a try. First I had a chat to the homeless guy, who was called Clive. We got on well together. He said he usually finished selling at three in the afternoon and was sure we could both make good money.

I was soon in a routine which started with a train journey to Victoria to buy a bundle of magazines, then back to Woolwich to sell them. Once I'd made about £20 I'd pack up for the day, go back to Gavin's and the two of us would go over the river to Silvertown, where Gavin had found a guy who did us a good deal on puff. We usually went by train because there was no one at Silvertown station so we travelled for free. Smack was easier to obtain. Ted and Sharon, who lived in a flat two storeys below us, used heroin on a daily basis and supplied us whenever we wanted a bit of gear. Gavin, who was a plasterer by trade, occasionally did a job 'cash in hand', and we'd treat ourselves to some gear.

Neither of us wanted to do any break-ins, but we did think about dealing from the flat. After lengthy discussions we admitted that it wouldn't work. With our track record, we would have smoked the stock before we'd had a chance to sell it. Not having a car made life more difficult and, in the end, we did have to do the break-ins. Most of the time we got by well enough on my sales of *The Big Issue* and Gavin's occasional bit of plastering. Gavin was able to afford a bed and the flat started to look more like home. Sales in Woolwich were going well, but by the end of the week those who were going to buy had done so, so on Saturdays I pitched up outside Tie Rack in Dartford. Between ten and two I would regularly sell twenty copies and the ladies in Tie Rack would change up my coins into notes. It turned out to be the best day of the week for me.

One day I came back and sat having a smoke with Gavin. We'd been wondering what was happening about the flat below us. Nobody seemed to live there. Gavin had had a word with Ted and Sharon who said that, as far as they knew, it had been unoccupied for some time. We decided to see if there was anything worth nicking. We rang the bell and waited. There was no answer. One hard kick and the door burst open. We went back along the landing and waited. Nobody opened their door to see what was going on, so we slipped into the empty flat. The furniture had seen better days and there was no stereo. We made a quick search, picking up the odd item, like a clock that we might be able to sell. I pulled the cushions from the armchair in the living room and there it was – a plastic bag stuffed with notes. We were out of there in an instant, back into Gavin's flat and counting.

With £400 burning a hole in our pockets, we set off for Silvertown straight away. Once we were back home we couldn't agree how to celebrate. I wanted to get really stoned. Gavin wanted to have a good drink up and a game of pool. We decided to give Ted and Sharon a knock so they could get some smack for me, and to ask William, who lived across the landing, to join Gavin for a game of pool. I said I'd come over to the pub for a couple of pints until Ted and Sharon had got the heroin, then I'd see Gavin back at the flat later on. We gave Ted and Sharon twenty quid for telling us about the flat and they had a drink in the pub with us, once they'd got the gear for me. Ted, Sharon and I left Gavin and William playing pool and made our way back to Ted's flat. I spent the night out of my head on drugs and went back to Gavin's place in the early hours. He wasn't there and there was no sign of him when I finally woke up. I wasn't worried because I thought he had probably picked up a girl and had gone home with her. As for me, I had plenty of puff left and I was soon into some heavy smoking.

It was around four in the afternoon when I heard the front door open. Someone called my name. I didn't recognize the voice so I got up to investigate. Two plainclothed policemen walked into the room. Gavin was handcuffed to one of them. There was an eighth of an ounce of puff on the table and one of the policemen kept his eye on that while the other went for 'a look around'. 'What's happened then?' I asked Gavin. 'Me and William got caught in a flat downstairs,' he started to explain. The policeman interrupted. 'Whose is that?' he inquired, indicating the puff. I told him it was mine. They found nothing else so they decided not to charge me, but they took my eighth away with them. Once they'd gone, I relaxed. It could have been worse. I'd done all that heroin in Ted's the night before and I had another quarter of an ounce of puff in my pocket. Added to which, for once there were no stolen video recorders or stereos in the flat. The police had been unlucky this time, I concluded, and I rolled a joint to celebrate.

Later that day Gavin was charged, then released on bail. He said he and William had decided to go back to the empty flat just in case we'd missed anything worth having. Someone had called the police and they'd been caught. I asked about my puff. Gavin said the policeman had dropped it down a drain outside. What a waste, but better than being charged.

It was summer and it was hot. I went out selling *The Big Issue* every day. Gavin started a training course in plastering, so it would look as though he was making an effort to live a decent life when he appeared in court. Geoff had finished his probation in the hostel and was living in a bedsit in Pimlico. All the time I was selling *The Big Issue*, I was signing on and stating that I had no fixed address, so if I got into any bother it would be difficult to track me down. As usual trouble was just around the corner.

I picked up my giro from the Social Security office in Woolwich and stopped to speak to Ted and

Sharon. They spent a lot of their time hanging around outside the office with a few others. On this particular day they were talking to a man I'd not seen before. They introduced him to me. His name was Willy and he'd just come out of prison. Willy was looking for a bit of puff and Ted asked if I could help him out. I was about to go to Silvertown, so I said he could come along with me. We got on well from the start, and I invited him back to Gavin's flat for a smoke. Gavin liked him too and for the next couple of weeks we saw him nearly every day.

Willy was good company usually, but one day he approached me as I was selling *The Big Issue* and he had a face like thunder. He had his and his wife's Staffordshire bull terriers with him and was on his way to the Social Security office. He said that, although he'd been released over two weeks ago, they still hadn't sorted him out any money, so he was going to sort them out! I'd taken a couple of Valium earlier that day and felt pretty dopey, so I decided to go with him in the hope that the walk would wake me up. I followed him inside to the desk, where he demanded to see someone. He was asked to wait. Willy exploded. 'I've been waiting two blinking weeks,' he roared, 'I want to see someone now.' After a few more heated exchanges the security guard came over. Willy hit him.

As we headed for the door, the dogs were jumping up and barking and a man got in Willy's way. He lashed out at him with one of the dog's leads. The bloke fell to the floor and I half tripped over him. As I struggled to keep my balance, I inadvertently kicked him. We got to the door just as the police arrived.

They grabbed Willy, threw him down and sat on him. I was about to walk off when someone shouted, 'He was with him as well!' I was grabbed by an officer from a second police car, which had squealed to a halt outside. Willy was handcuffed with his hands behind his back and was cursing and swearing nonstop. The police were getting heavy-handed with him. My hands were cuffed behind me too, but I kept quiet.

When the police van arrived, Willy was forced to lie face down on the floor, while I was told to sit on the bench. Four police officers clambered in after me. Two of them sat on Willy and started to twist his arm up his back until he screamed out in pain. 'You're out of order. He can't move, so why don't you leave him alone!' I shouted at the offending officers. Their response was to sling me on top of Willy and to give both of us a hard ride to the police station. They kept the cuffs on while we were searched, then asked if we'd behave if they removed them. They needed us to sign for the property they'd taken from us. By now we had both calmed down and I was glad to get the handcuffs off. They had left a deep imprint on my wrists, since they'd been done up tighter than necessary – a measure the police often took when arresting someone for violent behaviour. We were both charged with affray and I was also charged with assault. Willy was charged with GBH on the security guard and the man who got in his way, assaulting the police and having two dangerous dogs. Willy's biggest worry while we were on remand was that the dogs would be put down, but this charge was dropped.

He and I shared a cell while we were on remand and I got to know him well. He felt strongly that I should not have been arrested, and told the police that the incident was nothing to do with me. All I'd done was to accidentally kick a guy on the floor and they only had that person's word for it. No one else could back up his accusation of assault. Nevertheless, every time I asked for bail it was refused.

We were placed on remand in Belmarsh prison near Woolwich. Gavin visited a couple of times with some puff, but after that he couldn't afford to bring any more. Belmarsh is a fairly new prison. We were in the category B part which maintained high security. It was difficult to smuggle drugs in. The visiting room was arranged with long benches, divided by wooden boards which acted as barriers between the prisoners and their visitors. Any drugs would have to be passed over the top and with the screws watching every movement and cameras focused along the top of each board it was hardly worth trying. If the screws thought a visitor had attempted to pass you something, prisoners were put on closed visits, which meant they were seated behind a perspex screen and talked to their visitors through a telephone. The cell searches in Belmarsh took place more regularly than in other prisons, but although security was tight, the officers were, in general, more easy-going.

Willy suggested we put our names down to do the industrial cleaning course, as he'd done it before and liked the instructor. We were on remand for months and it helped to pass the time. He had spent years in prison and we swapped stories. Mine were mostly about smuggling in drugs and his about the many violent incidents he was involved in. We used our canteen money and the money we had sent in to buy a bit of puff from people on our wing, but we never had enough. Willy had only recently finished a sentence served in Belmarsh, so he knew several of the inmates and was able to borrow some puff until we got our canteen. We cut it into spots to make it go further and saved all our dog ends. It was hard going compared to the Verne which now, in retrospect, seemed like a holiday camp.

At last we were sentenced. I got eighteen months; Willy two and a half years. I felt particularly aggrieved. Willy had done all he could to keep me out of prison, but my long criminal record had gone against me. Talking to him about God, the Devil, Heaven and Hell, I reiterated my belief that I would go to Hell after I'd died. Willy, who claimed to be an atheist, said that if there was a God, he was meant to be the God of love. 'If so, he doesn't love me,' I responded bitterly. 'How d'you work that one out?' Willy asked. I explained how, since my last spell in prison, I'd sold *The Big Issue* to keep going and tried my best to keep out of trouble, yet I'd still ended up in jail. 'That's not God,' he replied firmly, 'that's the Devil having a laugh with you.'

We'd spent so many months on remand that I was nearing the end of my sentence. I only had eight weeks to go. Willy didn't know how much longer he would be in Belmarsh. He thought he might be shipped out at any time. We'd completed our cleaning course and I was on association with the wing cleaners as I'd been cleaning the corridors with my instructor and the other inmates on the course. It was not my wing's night for association, but I was entitled to be out of my cell as I'd been working. One of the screws came up to me and told me to go to my cell. I told him I'd been working. He repeated the order to me. I said I'd been cleaning the corridors, but he wasn't listening. 'Bang up or you'll be seeing the governor in the morning,' he threatened. He wasn't going to admit he was in the wrong and I wasn't going to give way. 'Nick me then,' I retorted, 'because I'm entitled to watch the telly and I'm staying out!'

The next morning I was put in solitary. After a couple of hours I was taken before the governor. I pleaded not guilty. The prison officer explained his actions by claiming that there were not enough staff on the wing for me to have association the previous evening. This was news to me, but it didn't help. The governor said I should have obeyed the officer and if I wanted to complain I'd have to go through the complaints procedure. He fined me a minimal amount and said I was to be released back on the wing later that day.

Back in my cell I started thinking about how unfair the whole prison system was and what I could do to show the screws that I was in the right. By the time they came to let me back on the wing, I had decided to stay on the block in protest and to demand to see the board of visitors. When an officer opened my cell door just before dinner I told him I was staying where I was on protest and I slammed the door shut. He opened the spy flap and said he'd give me one more chance. Again I told him I was not moving and I demanded to see the board. 'Please yourself then,' he said casually and walked off. They brought me my dinner and left me alone for the rest of the afternoon.

I spent that afternoon talking out of the window to the guy in the cell below me. The next day I was put on report for disobeying an order again. The governor fined me a week's wages and later that day the board of visitors came to see me. They spoke to me through the cell door and advised me to make an official complaint. I explained that by the time it was processed my discharge date would have come and gone, so I wanted the governor's decision overturned before I left the block. Unless I made the complaint, they told me, they could take it no further. In response, I told them I would carry on with my protest. Two days passed and I ran out of tobacco. Occasionally I sent down a line to the bloke in the cell below me and he attached a roll-up to it which just about kept me going.

I was bored out of my mind. Perhaps that was why I asked for a Bible when a screw put his head round the door and asked if I wanted anything. He brought me a Bible later that afternoon. I didn't know where to start with it, so I flicked through the first pages until I found a story I could recognize. It was about Noah's Ark and, as I read it, memories of Sunday School flooded back and triggered thoughts about my family. It shook me when I calculated that I'd not been in contact with my parents, brothers or sister for over ten years. I fell to thinking about Sunday School days again and I remembered Willy saying that it wasn't God who kept making me go back inside but the Devil having a laugh. When I woke up the next day I decided that my protest was pointless. The prison authorities would let me stay in the block until my discharge date came around, and nobody apart from the bloke in the cell below me and the officers on the block duty would even know that I had been on protest. When a screw came to my cell I told him I was ending my protest. He went away to fetch the Principal Officer, who asked me what had made me change my mind. I said I felt I wasn't achieving anything and that the board of visitors couldn't help. That afternoon they took me back to the wing. I walked out of the cell with my kit and left the Bible behind.

Within days Willy and I were on the move. He was sent to Albany prison on the Isle of Wight and I went to Blundestone prison in Suffolk. Although I had only eight weeks of my sentence left to serve, because of my protest they wanted me out. I promised Willy I'd visit him as soon as I was released and we said our goodbyes.

At Blundestone I found myself in a four-man cell. The other three had been there for some time. As I unpacked and looked around the cell I noticed a calendar from some church hanging on the wall. I felt tense and uncomfortable, but I didn't know why. I lay on the top bunk and got out the small amount of puff that Willy had given me before we left Belmarsh. I had enough for two joints and I needed them right away.

'Do you have a puff?' I asked nobody in particular. 'No, we've given that up now,' replied one of my cell mates. I went on rolling a joint and thought selfishly that at least I wouldn't have to share it. That first night was extremely quiet. There was very little by way of conversation and the following morning I thought I'd see about getting a cell change. One of the guys seemed to know what I was thinking. He told me to tell a prison officer that I smoked and then I should get a move. I asked who was the best screw to approach, but before anyone answered another cell mate, Deano, suggested that I stayed with him and the other two, Len and Brian.

Deano turned out to be really friendly, and he had had plenty of experience in smuggling heroin into jail. He'd used smack for years he said, but added, 'He got me off it.' 'Who was he?' I wanted to know. 'Jesus,' Deano replied. My response was a noncommittal 'Oh, yeah.' Nevertheless, two days in and I was getting on well with Deano and there was definitely a peaceful atmosphere in the cell. But one question niggled me. In the end I blurted it out. 'If you're all Christians,' I asked Deano, 'what are you doing in prison?' Deano explained that Len and Brian had turned away from their faith and returned to their old ways. 'Now they've been caught they want to change back again, I suppose,' I said cynically. Deano looked me in the eyes and said, 'God will never leave you or forsake you even if you slip up or turn away from him. And if you're really sorry he'll forgive you all over again.' He told me how he'd been saved in prison and had come off heroin without going cold turkey. I listened because this was one guy who knew what he was talking about when it came to drugs.

On Sunday I went to the church service with the others to maintain that peaceful atmosphere, but I found it boring and irrelevant. Deano and I talked a lot and he invited me to go to an evening meeting that Thursday. It would be different from the Sunday service, he assured me. It was taken by some Christians who lived locally and had no connection with the prison. I decided to give it a try. The leader was called Doug and there were some others, including Tina who was everybody's favourite and who always brought in little gifts. It felt friendly and relaxed. Doug shared something from the Bible which washed over me, but at the end of the meeting, we were asked to form a circle and hold hands while two or three people prayed. I'd never done such a thing in my life before and it seemed strange. Even having a coffee together afterwards was different, because it was the first time in all my years in prison that someone gave me a decent cup of coffee! It was the thought of that coffee that prompted me to go back the following Thursday!

The meeting began in much the same way, but because there weren't as many people there, Doug suggested that each of us should either talk a little about himself or about something we'd read in the Bible or wanted prayer for. Deano said a few words about how Jesus had helped him come off heroin. Meanwhile, I got the uncomfortable feeling that the rest of the group was waiting for me to say something, although nobody looked directly at me. Then, suddenly acting on impulse, I told everyone there what I really wanted to happen to me and why I knew it would never happen. I wanted my life to change, but I knew that with my track record I hadn't got a chance. My past would never leave me alone. Doug spoke to me as if I was the only one in that room.

Calmly and confidently he told me that when people turn to Jesus, he will forgive them, and even though we may remember our sins and those of other people, Jesus will forget them.

I wasn't convinced. 'That's well and good,' I responded, 'but I still don't see how you can change just like that.' Doug didn't answer me, but picked up his Bible and asked us to read Ephesians chapter six, verses ten to sixteen with him. It was all about God giving you armour, and at the end he asked me why I thought God would equip us with armour. 'The only reason I'd want it would be if I was going into battle,' I replied.

'Exactly,' said Doug. 'We're in a battle – not a flesh and blood one – but a spiritual battle.' He explained that we needed armour in our fight against the forces of wickedness. This was the first time I'd been shown the spiritual side of the Bible. Up till then I'd thought it was just a book of stories from time back. I'd never even thought about spiritual things, apart from when I read the odd Dennis Wheatley novel and that time in Devon when I went to aikido. That night I spent hours reading the Bible and the following Sunday afternoon I joined Doug for Bible study, as well as attending the morning service. I kept going to the Thursday meetings too and during one of these meetings I asked Jesus to sort my life out. The following week Tina gave me a Bible. On the inside front cover she'd written, 'Congratulations on your commitment, Tina.' I might have asked Jesus to sort out my life, but I didn't remember committing myself to anything. Still, I was pleased to have a Bible of my own.

When I was not in a service or a meeting I was rushing around the wing trying to get some drugs. I was finally allocated a job in the same shop as Brian. During our breaks, or when we were working at the same bench, we often talked about the Bible and at last, during those eight weeks at Blundestone, I began to feel that maybe I could change.

The drugs part of my life started to bug me. I thought that, if Deano could give up heroin after years of being on it, then I should be able to give up too. I told myself that, though I had used heroin a bit, there was no way I was addicted to it, and as for puff, that wasn't bad anyway. It wasn't addictive and I'd never heard of anyone ODing on it. So I told my cell mates that I was going to give up the hard drugs. Deano asked me why I didn't give them all up, but I insisted that there was nothing wrong with having a bit of puff. One evening we invited some new inmates to come for a chat in our cell. I boasted to them that I was giving up hard drugs and waited for them to congratulate me and tell me what a strong character I was. Instead, one of them, Oliver, gave me a warning look. He opened the Bible at Proverbs and read out a verse that said if you mock God you alone will suffer. I didn't know how to take Oliver. Did he think I was trying to take the mick out of him or was he genuinely trying to help me? I kept quiet, knowing how quickly an argument could escalate into a row.

My discharge date was coming up and I was told to go for an interview with the Principal Officer who was writing a discharge report on me. He said he'd noticed I'd been attending church regularly and then, to my surprise, asked: 'Would you say you have been born again?' My reply left no room for any doubts: 'No!'

As I packed my kit in the cell, I laid a calendar from the church on top of my few possessions. There was a quote from the Bible for each day and on my discharge date it said, 'I will visit you.' I remember pointing it out to Deano and saying, 'That's all right then. Look, God's going to be there when I get out so I don't have to worry about anything.' I took the Bible and the other bits Doug and Tina had given me, noted down the names and phone numbers of my cell mates, promised to keep in touch, then walked down the staircase to reception.

At last I was back in my own clothes, with £45 and my discharge papers in my pocket, plus a travel warrant that I exchanged at the local station for a rail ticket to Woolwich. I was planning to stay in Gavin's flat again, so I got off at Woolwich Dockyard and walked to his flat hoping that he'd be in. Ted and Sharon were coming out of the block as I arrived and took me straight up to their place. I told them I was giving up hard drugs, but since it was my first day out they fixed me up with a new works and some heroin. After having a hit, my mind started to work overtime on how I could get a bit more gear and manage to buy enough to eat for the week. I decided that if I kept back £10, I could get some *Big Issues* the next day and earn some money selling them. I asked Ted and Sharon if we could go and get some gear and spent that first night of freedom on their pull-out bed. I stayed with them for the next two weeks, selling *The Big Issue* by day and spending every penny I made on heroin.

Standing on the street corner one day with copies of *The Big Issue* draped over one arm, the thought suddenly struck me, 'This isn't for me.' I knew that if I carried on with the heroin I would soon end up with a serious habit. I had to do something, and quickly. I found myself a room and moved out of Ted's place. I spent my spare time with Gavin just having a drink and a bit of puff. I worked at selling *The Big Issue* as if it was my regular job. People would stop and talk and at the end of the day I'd have a meal, then share a puff and a few cans with Gavin at his place or mine. Within ten days I had got over the worst of the craving for heroin, and though my new home was only furnished with a couple of items of old furniture, I felt that I was taking control of my life at last.

Nine

A New Life

I'd had my own place for three weeks and was doing my usual trip to Victoria to pick up my copies of *The Big Issue* when I bumped into Geoff Hunter, who'd been in the hostel with Gavin and me. We went for a cup of tea and he told me he'd been given a bedsit in Pimlico, but he didn't need it because he'd moved in with his girlfriend in Chalk Farm. Geoff said I could rent the bedsit from him if I wanted and I jumped at the chance. Gavin was pleased because it meant he had somewhere to stay when he came into London, and I knew I was still welcome at his flat in Woolwich whenever I felt like a change.

I moved in at the end of the week and on the Monday took over Geoff's pitch at Victoria coach station, selling *The Big Issue* from 8 am to 10 am and then from 2 pm to 4 pm. Geoff put me in touch with people I could buy puff from and told me that his girlfriend, Kylie, could supply with me with hard drugs whenever I wanted them. She was getting drugs on prescription and sold them on the streets, so she knew just about every drug dealer around. Most evenings I went to her place or she and Geoff came to mine and we would drink a few ciders, smoke puff and chat. It also became a habit for Kylie to give me a couple of Valium to help me sleep.

Although the coach station was a good pitch, I also travelled round to different parts of London selling the magazine. I became quite familiar with the city streets and learned where *The Big Issue* sold well and where it didn't. One day, in the late summer, I found my way to Shepherd's Bush. It was very hot and after two hours standing across the road from the station I'd only managed to sell two copies. I sat down on the pavement in disgust and put the magazines in a heap beside me. I was thinking about where I should go next, when an ice cream was thrust in front of my face and a woman's voice said, 'I'm giving you this in the name of Jesus.' I took the ice cream and stumbled to my feet, but the woman was already half way down the road.

Some time after this incident, a traffic warden came over to me and invited me to his church. He said one of the church members would be able to help me find some accommodation. I told him I already had somewhere to stay. He moved on and I took up my pitch at the coach station. I'd made up a little rhyme, '*Big Issue* 70p: if not, a smile will do for me.' I repeated it every time a likely purchaser walked towards me, and I was saying it when a woman approached me and asked straight out, 'How do you stand with God?' I gave an instant answer to this strange and unexpected question. 'Not very good, I suppose.' Then she asked me if I wanted to go to a nearby café for a coffee and to say a prayer. I was all for a free cup of coffee and there was no harm in saying a prayer, so we went round the corner to a café called The Well.

Once we'd got our coffee, she introduced herself as Meg and asked me about my relationship with Jesus. I told her I knew about him but I didn't go to church. Then she asked me if I knew I was a sinner. I nearly fell off my chair laughing. 'I've got enough sins to fill a book,' I told her. 'Do you want to start writing it?'

I did tell Meg how I'd become interested in the Bible when I was finishing off my last prison sentence and, as we finished our coffee, she said she'd like to pray with me. She explained that it would be a sinner's prayer, asking Jesus to forgive me my sins and to make me clean through his death on the cross for me. I said I was ready and the prayer went like this, 'Dear Lord Jesus, I come to you as a sinner and ask you to forgive me my sins. I believe you are the Son of God who died and rose again on the third day. Wash me and cleanse me by the power of your blood. Help me to start a new life with you and follow you in your ways. Today I receive you as my Lord and Saviour. In Jesus' name, Amen.'

It was 16 August 1995 when I said that prayer with Meg and meant it. It was a day I will remember for the rest of my life. At last I acknowledged to myself that I couldn't sink much lower, and that the drink and drugs were just my way of trying to escape from the reality of my life.

Meg gave me her address and the name of an hotel where she and her friends held a Sunday service. She told me that on Friday nights they met outside McDonalds in Victoria Street to sing and give out leaflets. After she left the café I put the slip of paper with all the details on it in my pocket and went back to my pitch hoping to sell more copies of *The Big Issue*. At the end of the afternoon, instead of going to the off-licence for my usual cans of cider, I went back home and searched through my bags to find the Bible Tina had given me in prison. In the two months since my release I'd forgotten all I learned in the Bible studies at Blundestone. I spent the night looking through the Bible, trying to find something to read that I would understand. For some reason Geoff and Kylie didn't call round that evening, so I was uninterrupted, but when morning came, I concluded that the Bible still didn't make much sense to me.

Two days later I gave it another go, but it was hopeless. I read the words on the page, but they meant nothing to me. I decided to go and see Meg and ask for her help. I scrubbed my jeans in the bath and washed my shirt, thinking that, if I was going to this Christian woman's nice home, I'd better make an effort. My bedsit was like me, not dirty but a bit of a mess.

I called at the address Meg had given me and the door was answered by a guy of about twenty. He looked as scruffy as me and it occurred to me that I might have the wrong address, but he confirmed that Meg lived there and I followed him into the flat. There was no carpet on the floor and the furniture was as tatty as mine, but Meg's welcome was warm and sincere. She was staying at the flat which belonged to Mel, the bloke who'd let me in.

As Meg prepared some soup, I chatted to Mel and discovered that he'd experienced plenty of tough times. He'd been homeless and spent long stretches in hospitals for the mentally ill. He'd been living rough when he became a Christian only seven weeks earlier, and in that brief time his life had been radically changed. He'd even succeeded in giving up smoking, something I wanted to do but wouldn't admit to! The four of us talked about the Bible and at the end of the evening Meg reminded me that they'd be outside McDonalds in Victoria Street the next evening. If I couldn't join them there, she added, she'd love me to call around on Sunday and go to church with them.

That Friday evening I stayed in, expecting Geoff to turn up. As I waited I read the stories in the Bible I remembered from Sunday School days. Before I realized it two hours had passed and there was no sign of Geoff, so I decided to go to Victoria Street and have a chat with Meg. There was a group of about ten outside McDonalds. They'd set up a generator to power an electric guitar and a mike and soon the singing was in full swing. I offered to help give out leaflets, but I didn't have any takers! Back in my bedsit I smoked a few joints, then had one pipe of puff before crashing out.

The next morning, after a breakfast of cornflakes and a pipe, I rolled the rest of my puff in a two skinner joint, then collected twenty copies of *The Big Issue* and bought a ticket to Dartford. On an average Saturday I'd sell all the copies and take about £20. This Saturday, when I went into Tie Rack to change up my cash, I found I'd taken £35. That was enough to buy puff for myself and for Willy who was still in prison. On the way home I decided to stop off in

Deptford and visit Ken who'd been in prison with us. He'd always said that if I was going to see Willy, he'd give me a bit of puff on top to take in for him. When I got to Ken's flat he was so drunk he could hardly stand up and he hadn't got any puff. I told him not to worry, I'd get some in Victoria.

When I reached Victoria, I headed straight for the tube and made my way to Geoff and Kylie's. They told me they hadn't been to see me because Geoff had been ill for a week. He still looked pretty bad and I didn't stay long because they weren't able to supply me with any puff and I needed to get some sorted out because I wanted to go and see Willy the next day. I went to every dealer I knew in the Chalk Farm area, but they were either out or didn't have anything to sell me. I went back to Victoria and tried my regular supplier, the bloke in the flat below me. There was no answer. I went to the nearest phone box and started to ring around.

Finally, I got through to a guy who said he'd call round with some puff. Two hours went by and he still hadn't turned up. I called him again. No reply. I tried his mobile. It was switched off. I rang every half an hour, always with the same result. It was like going to the pub and not being able to buy a drink. I was angry and on edge because I couldn't even have a joint myself. I crawled into bed feeling that the whole world had let me down.

Sunday morning dawned, and I had to get some puff before ten o'clock when the coach left for the Isle of Wight and Albany prison. I tried the guy downstairs and the one who'd promised to come round. Neither responded, so I gave up on the plan to go and see Willy, and decided instead to visit the church Meg had talked about. I called at Mel's flat and we walked together to a hotel where the Holy Nation Church held its services. It seemed a strange venue, but it was very friendly and informal.

The pastor welcomed everyone there, especially first timers, and he seemed to be looking straight at me when he said it. Then the congregation launched into song, accompanied by people on the electric keyboard and guitar. I didn't know what they were singing, but there was one easy one called 'We are the winners' and I joined in. When we sang the line 'Satan defeated, Hallelujah!' I suddenly felt at peace. Tears rolled down my cheeks. By the time the singing ended I had a smile on my face and joy in my heart. I remember nothing of the sermon that day, but after the service Meg gave me an audio tape and asked me to listen to it at home.

I slipped the tape into the deck and listened through headphones. A man called Ian McCormack told his story. He was stung by four box jelly fish while swimming in the Indian Ocean. The medical team worked hard, but Ian was pronounced dead and efforts at resuscitation ceased. Fifteen minutes later, to the shocked delight of those present, he revived. His tape, called *A Glimpse of Eternity* is an account of those fifteen minutes during which he was shown part of Heaven and Hell. I was so engrossed by Ian's story that I lost all sense of time and place. When the tape finished and I came back down to earth, I realized that I hadn't even had a roll-up that day. I picked up my tobacco and a packet of Rizlas and made one. After two drags, I nearly threw up.

'That's going to have to go,' I thought to myself and I took the tobacco to the rubbish chute outside my bedsit and threw it out. As I walked back inside, tears trickled down my face and the Holy Spirit filled my heart. I threw out my ashtrays and the empty cider cans, and made a decision to clean up the bedsit and sort myself out.

I went to the church office the next day and joined in the morning prayer. Everyone was praying in tongues, which was new to me but I wasn't bothered by it. I just knelt down and asked Jesus to help me sort out my life. I told the pastor I wanted to be rid of all the hash pipes and bongs, including the ones which belonged to Geoff. The pastor advised me not to throw away someone else's property, and suggested I returned Geoff's stuff to him. I was worried that if I went round to Geoff's I might be tempted to buy some drugs off him, so I put his bits into a carrier bag and stored them in a cupboard.

I was full of energy, like having a hit of speed. At three in the morning, I was chucking away pornographic magazines along with everything else I felt was bad. Even my little puff pipe that I had smoked every night before going to bed had to go. It was an act of repentance, although I didn't know it at the time. That evening I had dinner at Mel's flat, and when I got home I wrote to Willy. I told him about my plan to visit, how I'd been unable to buy puff anywhere and what had happened when I went to church instead of the Albany prison. I explained about feeling washed clean, which reminded me of the time when Georgy had visited me in the Verne, and I said I'd changed and hoped Willy would too.

Finally I said I couldn't get up to visit him and that I'd given up taking drugs, but was sending him a postal order for £10 and would send him some more money when I could.

I put Willy's letter aside and took a fresh piece of paper. I wrote, 'Dear Mum and Dad' and stopped. What should I write? 'I know I haven't contacted you for ten tears but I've just met Jesus!' I tried to think it through. Did they still live at the same address? Were they still both alive? Would they believe I'd changed? I crumpled up the piece of paper and threw it in the bin. Writing to them was a crazy idea. I began to have doubts about sending Willy's letter. Perhaps I should go and see him instead. I decided to sleep on it.

I was up at 6 am saying my prayers for the third morning in a row. As I prayed I started to cry, but afterwards I was full of energy again. I leapt into the bath and said out loud, 'Lord you've cleaned me inside, I'll clean the outside.' After my bath and breakfast, I got to work on the bedsit. I was cleaning the windows when the postman came, and I smiled and said 'Good morning' to him. He smiled at me and said 'Good morning' back. Such a simple, unremarkable exchange and yet it felt like the best morning of my life. An hour or so later, as I was on my way to buy my copies of *The Big Issue*, I found the list of drug dealers' phone numbers in my pocket. I ripped it up and dumped it in a bin.

I arrived for morning prayers at the church office and joined the small group who gathered there at ten every day. Some of them would go out on the streets afterwards, preaching and singing. Meg worked on the computer, and Sophie cleaned the office and made drinks. Before I left for my pitch I showed my letter to Willy to the pastor. He thought I should send it, but I said nothing about the letter to my parents, although it was constantly on my mind.

When I returned to my bedsit, having sold my quota of *The Big Issue*, I realized that Geoff and Kylie hadn't been over since I met Meg. I laughed out loud as I pictured Geoff's face if he saw the state of the bedsit now. It was spotlessly clean and tidy. That night I prayed that God would give me the gift of tongues. Something welled up inside me, and a faint noise seemed to flow out of me from my throat, but nothing else happened. I went to bed feeling totally relaxed and at peace. It was very different the next morning. When I tried to repeat the experience I was almost physically sick. Determined to carry on, I knelt with my head over the toilet! I kept retching, as if I was going to vomit, but after a few minutes I felt better. At morning prayer it happened again. As I prayed, I shook and retched, but I didn't stop. Suddenly I felt full of energy. The words flowed and afterwards I realized that God had given me the gift I'd asked for.

A few of us went off to Little Ben. Mel took the mike and told how Jesus had saved him, then I spoke in public for the first time ever. I was brief and to the point. I said I knew nothing, except Christ and that he was crucified for me. Just three days ago I was doing drugs, but now Jesus had set me free. From being a prisoner I'd become a preacher! After that first experience of speaking on the streets, I went out regularly with the others, giving my testimony and handing out leaflets. I used to keep some of these on display in the bedsit, and when I found a sticker Tina had given me in Blundestone prison I stuck it on the bare light bulb. It was yellow with a smiley face printed on it and the words 'Smile, Jesus loves you.'

The next day I met the man who had been led to set up the Holy Nation Church. His name was Pastor Kunle Omilana, and he and his wife Rebecca had just returned from America. I poured out my story to him and he listened intently. I hadn't the faintest idea about church planting or how churches are organized, all I knew was that here was another person who not only had time for me but valued me too.

I was back in Dartford selling *The Big Issue*, at my usual Saturday pitch, when I collapsed. The woman from Tie Rack phoned for an ambulance. She thought I was having an epileptic seizure. I woke in hospital and the medical staff told me they could find nothing wrong with me, and no reason why I'd lost consciousness so dramatically. I told the doctor I'd recently become a Christian, and maybe I'd been delivered from something demonic. He told me he'd heard of such occurrences but discharged me with a clean bill of health. It has never happened since and may have been my body's reaction to being totally cut off from drugs.

When I returned to my bedsit after the evening service the following day, I wrote that letter to my parents and posted it to the last address I knew of, hoping they hadn't moved in the intervening decade. With that accomplished, I took the carrier bag of pipes and bongs over to Chalk Farm. I sat in Kylie's flat explaining to Geoff what had happened in my life. The more I talked, the more annoyed he became. When I said I'd thrown out everything I had to do with drugs, he said he wished I'd given them to him instead as he'd have found a use for them. He tersely brought the conversation to a close, saying he'd come over to collect the rent once a week.

Although losing Geoff as a friend didn't bother me too much, when I received a letter from Willy the next morning all the joy and energy my new life had given me drained away. The gist of the letter was that he thought I was a strong personality, not the type to be swayed by religion. He said I'd let him down and he was in debt because I hadn't come with the drugs. What really hurt me, though, was his statement: 'Don't try and convert me or I'll grow to hate you.'

He told me not to show his letter to anyone in the church, but I was feeling so bad about it that I took it to one of the blokes I went out witnessing with. He read it and said he would help me write a reply if I wanted him to. After morning prayers I came to a decision. I wouldn't write back to Willy. Any debts he'd incurred were down to him, not me. Once again I thought of Georgy telling me he'd become a Christian, and how I'd told him that he was wasting a visit by not bringing in any drugs. If a friendship was based solely on drugs, I concluded, it wasn't a genuine friendship. Pastor Mike confirmed my feelings. He read Willy's letter and afterwards said that when we decide to follow Jesus, there will be some things and some people whom we have to leave behind us. We shouldn't forget them, but should go on praying for them. As I went off to sell *The Big Issue*, I ripped up Willy's letter and threw it in the bin.

My tattoos were another worry. I had heard that Satan can attack where there are demonic signs, but I hadn't a chance of raising enough money to have them removed. Some of the people at church put my mind at rest. They told me that when we come to Jesus Christ, he breaks every curse or stronghold that Satan has over us, because Jesus came to destroy the works of the Devil. Meg prayed with me and denounced all the bad things connected with the tattoos. Now I use the tattoos to show that Jesus can indeed triumph over the Devil and turn a person's life around.

Satan doesn't give up easily. For me the battle had only just begun. I started to settle in my new routine – daily morning prayers with Mel, Meg, Sophie, Wally and Pastor Mike; preaching on the streets twice a week and selling *The Big Issue* every day except for Sunday. But nothing stays the same. Meg had to leave London and I felt that, just as I had found a true friend who really cared about me, God was sending her away. We held a going-away party for Meg, and the following night I sat alone in my bedsit with a couple of cans of cider. Looking round, I thought of all the stuff I'd thrown out. Without Meg, I mused, it was all for nothing. There was a knock on the door. I knew it would be Meg, but I wouldn't let myself open the door. She kept knocking and I could hear her calling 'Mick', but I didn't move out of my chair. In the end she gave up and left. When I woke up the next morning I felt empty. I went to the church office, and as I prayed I realized that Satan had robbed me of the joy of saying goodbye to Meg at the station. The Bible says that Satan is a thief who comes to kill, steal and destroy, and I had just found out that what he wants to steal from you most isn't possessions but love, peace and happiness. That morning I recovered the joy in my life.

I decided to leave the bedsit and move in with Mel. I went to Chalk Farm to tell Geoff that I was moving out at the end of the week. I had the distinct impression that he wanted me out anyway. I told him I'd cleaned it up and when he came to pick up the keys he was visibly impressed with what I'd done. I'd already shifted all my belongings to Mel's flat so I walked away leaving only one small reminder of my time there – a sticker on the light bulb saying, 'Smile, Jesus loves you!'

Ten

Mission to Albania

A few months after I'd moved in with Mel, Pastor Kunle suggested that Mel and I went with him on a mission trip to Albania. I searched through my things for my passport and discovered that it had expired. It appeared to be only valid for one year, although I'd paid for a ten-year passport before I went off to Jamaica. Mel had never been abroad before, and he was as excited as me about our proposed trip. When we told Wally the news, he said he felt God wanted him to go to Germany as he kept meeting German people on the streets. Wally seemed to have a funny idea about how God spoke to him, but he wasn't a bad bloke and the three of us had some good times together.

When Mel and I arranged to go to the Passport Office, Wally decided he should get a passport as well so that he'd be ready to go abroad at any time. I got the impression that Wally was upset that he wasn't coming with us, and although I said nothing, Pastor Kunle must have picked up on this, because he told Wally that he could come too as long as he acquired a passport. Mel and I had all the paperwork and photos we needed, but Wally kept hitting snags and required constant help. Together, we managed to find an appropriate person to sign the back of his photos and sorted out adequate identification for him. At the Passport Office my passport was renewed and Mel was told he'd receive his in a couple of days' time. As for Wally – somehow he'd managed to lose his forms of ID on the way so he couldn't apply for his passport. Over the next two or three weeks Wally came up with several different excuses which prevented him from getting a passport. Pastor Kunle told Mel and me not to worry about it, and one Sunday he preached about the fear of going forward. Perhaps this was Wally's problem, I thought to myself. Whereas Mel and I were ready to step out into the unknown if we believed that was what God wanted us to do, others would hold back and resist any promptings to go forward with God.

The final arrangements for the trip to Albania were made. There would be five of us travelling in Christine's small car. Wally's replacement was a lady called Barbara. She was bringing bags of clothes to give away to the Albanians and with this, plus boxes of tracts in English and Albanian, we had to limit ourselves to one holdall each.

A few days before we left, Mel met a guy on the streets called Adam and brought him back to stay in the flat. Adam really wanted to get his life straightened out. Although he was homeless, he'd managed to land a job as a kitchen porter and, despite washing up all day, he was keen to help with the housework in the flat. He was easy to get on with and Mel believed he was sleeping rough through no fault of his own. We decided to ask Wally to stay with Adam in the flat while we were away and gave him the one and only door key.

At last the big day came and we set out for Dover, having squeezed ourselves and our luggage into Christine's Volkswagen Golf. It was a relief to get out of the car once we were on Eurostar, but many long hours of being squashed in the back of the Golf lay ahead! We made good time, arriving in Paris in the afternoon. We had something to eat in McDonalds, then started looking for a reasonably priced hotel. On our way to collect the car, I stopped to speak to a woman wrapped in a blanket and sheltering in a phone box. I wanted to tell her that Jesus had a better way for her, but I was greeted with a stream of abuse. She told me in no uncertain terms where to go. I try not to become disheartened when people react like her, but it's hard.

At last we came across a hotel called Victoria. It had to be the place to stay! We booked in, and woke the next morning ready to start another day. Pastor Kunle suggested that we spent our time evangelizing in Paris. Although we were booked in on a room-only basis, the hotel allowed us to help ourselves to breakfast and didn't charge. We spent the day giving out tracts and talking to people. As we walked around, we came across some children who looked as though they were homeless. They said they slept in the subways. We could do little for them as we had no connections with any churches in Paris or homeless organizations, but before we left the city that evening, we took them for a meal.

As we drove through the city streets, we discussed the possibility of going to Paris once a month to evangelize. We'd enjoyed our short time there and felt compelled to go back again soon. We were so busy talking, that it was ages before we realized that we were getting nowhere other than totally lost. Christine could not find her way out of Paris. Pastor Kunle pointed out that we had forgotten to remain united and focused. Some of us wanted to go on with our mission to Albania. Others wanted to stay in Paris.

Christine pulled over and we prayed that we would have a common purpose, then set off again. Just up the road, Christine slowed down, unsure of which turning to take at the next junction. The car behind us overtook and drew up alongside us. The driver asked in perfect English if we needed help. When Christine explained where we wanted to go, he gave her the directions she needed, and from then on we had no problem getting out of Paris and finding the road that would take us to the border with Italy.

Christine drove through the night. I kept dozing and waking. Pastor Kunle stayed awake talking to Christine, who got no rest yet didn't seem to tire. Day broke and the journey continued. I spent a lot of time reading, and asking the Pastor to explain bits that I didn't understand. The accident happened just before the turn-off to Vonce, where we planned to stop before going on to Albania. Christine missed the sign which indicated a road joining from the left. The car which sped down that road had the right of way. Christine braked, but too late. There was the frightening sound of metal buckling under the impact of metal.

Once both vehicles had skidded to a halt, we got out to check that the passengers in the other car were unhurt. There were two adults and two children and they were all fine. The offside door of their car was badly dented, but they stayed calm and drove off with our insurance details and no bad feelings. The Golf had sustained a small dent in the wing, but no other damage. We set off again and soon arrived at Vonce, which was only a twenty-minute drive from Nice. Christine turned off the main road and drove up a narrow winding lane to the villa where we were going to spend the next couple of days.

I got out of the car, stretched and looked around. It was a beautiful place. Behind me were snow-peaked mountains and, because we were quite high up, Vonce lay spread out beneath us like a toy town. Bruno, who looked after the villa, made us most welcome, and when I woke up the next morning I felt at peace with God. I slipped out of the villa and sat on the steps outside, reading aloud from my Bible. Strangely, I didn't feel silly or awkward – it was as if I were reading the passage to another person although I was on my own. The local people were friendly and life carried on at a gentle pace. It was so different from London, where everyone rushed around and got annoyed if you didn't move fast enough. That evening, friends of Christine invited us to a meal and their hospitality was overwhelming.

After two days of rest, we were on the move again, with a drive across the mountains and into Italy. As we headed for the mountain road, we noticed smoke coming from the rear of the car. We stopped and discovered oil was leaking onto the back axle. There was a garage nearby, so Christine and Pastor Kunle went to ask for help. When they returned they looked serious. The garage couldn't do repairs and said we'd need to take the car to a Volkswagen specialist. The Pastor suggested that we should pray about the situation. We must have looked a strange sight to passing motorists as we stood round the car and prayed! We set off again. I kept looking out of the window to see if any black smoke was billowing up from the wheels, but Pastor Kunle told me it would be all right and, sure enough, there was not a whiff of smoke to be seen.

We were so carried away with our faith drive that we forgot to fill up with petrol before driving over the mountains. It was during the early hours of the morning and we were already quite a way across the mountains, when someone noticed the fuel gauge was hovering just above the empty sign. As we drove through tunnel after tunnel and round the twisting, bendy roads, the fuel in the tank was rapidly used up. Finally it ran out. Once again we prayed about the situation. I said nothing out loud, but I was thinking – what do the others believe will happen now? Do they reckon the petrol tank will suddenly register full?

To my relief, once we'd finished praying, Mel walked to the emergency phone and rang for help. It was a long wait and when the guy finally turned up he had no petrol for us. Instead he put the car on the back of his truck and drove to the nearest town. We tried to talk to him on the way, but his English was poor, and he showed no interest in the tract we gave him. When we reached the town, Christine asked him to stop so she could get some money out of a cashpoint machine to pay him. She came back to the cab of the breakdown truck with a long face. For some reason there were insufficient funds in her account. She couldn't pay the bloke. He exploded into a storm of angry words which we, fortunately, couldn't understand! Then he drove to his garage, unloaded the Golf, and slung the tract he'd been given into Mel's face. Finally, he parked his truck across the entrance so we were blocked in.

I felt like walking out and hitch-hiking back to England. The bloke kept marching in and out of his garage, shouting and mouthing off at us. Pastor Kunle reacted in his usual way. He asked us all to get in the car and pray with him. I was still working out how far it would be to hitch-hike home when I heard the Pastor say, 'Thank you Lord,' as if it was all sorted out. He turned to Christine and asked her to go to the bloke, and tell him that we would send him the money we owed as soon as we were back in England. Christine did so, but the man wanted to keep her passport. Pastor Kunle sent her back, and she told him she couldn't hand over her passport because of our mission to Albania. This time she came back to the car with the garage bloke, who had had a sudden change of heart. He was smiling and co-operative and happily filled the tank with petrol, taking our word that he would be paid for all he'd done as soon as it was possible. He didn't even ask for something to be left with him as surety.

We made it to Italy with no further problems and booked into a hotel for the night. The next day we drove to Bari, intending to take the ferry to Albania. There were a couple of hours to kill before the ferry departed, so we decided to explore the port area. Mel and I went one way, Pastor Kunle, Christine and Barbara another. After a wander round, Mel and I returned to keep an eye on the car. It was parked by the water's edge and we sat nearby enjoying the fresh air and watching people fishing.

About half an hour before the ferry was due to sail a security man approached us and asked what we were waiting for. We told him we were waiting for the ferry and for our friends. He asked us to accompany him to the office, where we were questioned by his superior. This man seemed to be particularly interested in Pastor Kunle, and when Mel said he didn't know how long it would be before the Pastor joined us, he became incensed. He asked me the same question and I replied, 'Me no understand.' This is a favourite saying with foreign tourists in England so I thought I'd try it out. My response infuriated the officer even more. He threatened to break my bones, then he dragged Mel off into another room. They returned five minutes later and he said we could go.

We went back to the car, thinking that perhaps they suspected us of trying to smuggle drugs, although they hadn't attempted to search the car. By the time the others got back, we were already queuing for the ferry. When I told Pastor Kunle about our interrogation he appeared to be unconcerned and we duly drove onto the ferry and sat in the car waiting for the other vehicles to board. Suddenly two men appeared and demanded to see our passports. Having checked them, they said that Mel, Christine and I could continue our journey, but Pastor Kunle and Barbara would not be allowed into Albania because they didn't have visas. We explained that we couldn't split up because Christine was the only one with access to cash through her credit card. The men weren't interested. They decided they wanted all five of us off the ferry. Boarding had been halted, and they gestured to four men dressed in orange overalls to come over to our car. It was clear that, one way or another, they were going to get us off that ferry. Mel leapt out of the car and stood defensively in front of the bonnet. In a loud voice he proclaimed that we were going to Albania in Jesus' name, but it cut no ice with the customs officers. Pastor Kunle's negotiations failed too, so we had to drive off the ferry.

We booked into a hotel for the night and spent the rest of that frustrating day telling people the good news in the town. The next day we put plan B in action. Pastor Kunle and Barbara would fly to Albania while the rest of us took the ferry. We drove to the airport and Pastor Kunle went in to sort out flights for himself and Barbara. He returned to the car empty-handed. The same official who stopped us at the ferry was at the airport. Tickets were refused. We weren't going to make it to Albania. I was devastated. As far as I was concerned, we'd failed on our mission. Pastor Kunle had a different view of the situation. He pointed out that God was able to turn everything around for good, but I was too downhearted to be comforted. We drove back to town to find somewhere to eat, but I opted to stay in the car and sleep. The others did their best to persuade me to go with them, but I wasn't going anywhere. All I wanted to do was to curl up on the back seat and wallow in my own misery. After about an hour they returned with a pizza for me. This cheered me up a bit, because it reminded me that I was with people who cared about me. I realized that becoming a Christian wasn't just about going to church on a Sunday, and having an easy, carefree life, nor was going on a mission trip a form of holiday. There would be a lot of low points, times when everything seemed to go wrong, but when we had the joy of the Lord with us it made it all worthwhile.

It had been a bad day, but I put it behind me. The next day was Sunday. We tried to attend a church we'd noticed in the town a day or two before, only to find it closed. This setback didn't seem to matter too much. God has his own agenda and that day we found a pastor and his wife who not only invited us into their home but asked us to stay. Pastor Kunle had found the phone number of their church and rang to ask about the times of their services. That phone call led to us staying with them for over a week, giving us the opportunity to evangelize in Bari down by the railway station. We used tracts from their church printed in Italian. Although I couldn't understand a word, handing them out helped to break the ice and if anyone wanted to talk, I could direct them to a person from the church or even Christine who has the gift of being able to pick up foreign languages easily and quickly. Since there was an American base in Bari, we were able to bring the message of salvation to many GIs.

Two days later, the pastor's wife asked Mel and I if we would share our testimonies at a house group. She explained that most of the women in the group were married to men who were involved in drug dealing. I told my story and at the end I asked the women to keep praying for their husbands, because if Jesus could forgive me, he could forgive anyone. When Mel shared his testimony of what it was like in hospitals for the mentally ill, describing how he had drugs forced into him against his will, one woman wept openly. Her reaction put all the problems we'd had in attempting to go to Albania into perspective. God had used us to speak to this one person and that made everything worthwhile.

All too soon it was time to leave. We had had such a wonderful time there that I think I left a little bit of myself behind when we set off on the long journey back to London. The drive home was incident free and I was looking forward to saying a few words about our trip at the Sunday morning service. I was going to talk about the oil leak and how we had driven all the way to Italy and back without having to have any repairs done.

It was very late when Mel and I got back to his flat. We knocked on the door, but no one responded. At first we thought that Wally and Adam were asleep, so we knocked even louder, and shouted through the letter box. It became obvious that the flat was unoccupied. As we'd given Wally the one and only key, we had the choice of either breaking in or calling out an emergency locksmith. The front door was quite solid – too difficult to kick in, and the windows were double glazed with diamond-shaped leading. I no longer owned my special set of keys, so I couldn't pick the lock and we decided to call out the locksmith. When he turned up, he smashed some glass in the top of the door and reached down to open the door from the inside. I was annoyed because I could have done that myself, but had wanted to avoid causing too much damage. The locksmith nailed a board over the broken pane of glass and left, just as we discovered that there was no power in the flat. We had to go across to the night garage and charge up the key. It seemed that we had trusted Wally with the flat and he'd abused that trust. With the lights back on, we found the door key lying on the table in the front room. Why had he left it there? I wondered. He could have given it to Pastor Mike, who would have made sure there was someone to let us in on our return.

A few days passed before I caught up with Wally. He said Adam had come back drunk one night so he'd asked him to leave. Then some days later he'd gone out and forgotten to take the key, so he'd locked himself out. He claimed he'd had to sleep on the streets. I told him I didn't think he should have kicked Adam out, and that it was strange that he hadn't let Pastor Mike know what was going on. Despite what had happened, Mel and I still invited Wally round for a meal and let him sleep on the sofa for a night or two. Then I met Adam on the streets. He told me that he hadn't got drunk – Wally just threw him out. His story rang true, and I told him he was welcome to see me and Mel anytime he wanted, but soon my attitude towards the waifs and strays who came to the flat began to change. I didn't know it then, but I was about to go through months of misery and torment.

Eleven

Backsliding

Mel was happy to open up the flat to anyone. He'd often come home with someone he'd found sleeping rough and he'd let them stay for as long as they wanted. Once Mel and I started preaching at them, they usually stayed for no more than two nights! With lots of overnight 'lodgers' and Mel's tendency to be messy and untidy, I found myself constantly clearing up and making the flat habitable. In time it got to me. I resented sharing the flat with others and wanted it to be just for Mel and myself, but when I tried to tell Mel about how I felt he didn't take any notice. He kept bringing people back to the flat.

One couple he came home with, Reggie and Patsy, brought the tension in the flat to breaking point. It started with Reggie and me sharing a bedroom while Mel and Patsy slept in the sitting room. Soon they began to complain that by keeping them apart, we were attempting to break up their relationship. They kept on at Mel, recognizing that he was a soft touch, and after a few weeks he gave in and let them sleep in the same room. Once they'd won this battle, they stuck their heels in and refused to go to church with us or pray or even get out of bed at a reasonable time.

I stopped selling *The Big Issue* and found myself a cleaning job. I began work at midnight at The Marche restaurant with a small team of cleaners. Each team member had a set number of tasks to complete, and could go home when they'd finished. My main task was to scrub the floor, but I was able to do it quite quickly, as I had a machine to do all the hard work. Rather than go back to the flat right away, I usually stayed to help the others finish their tasks. It gave me an opportunity to tell them about Jesus and what he had done in my life. I soon discovered that one of the women cleaners was a Christian and another guy was interested, so the three of us turned up to work fifteen minutes early every night, so we could pray together. As time went on the non-Christians on the team moved on and were replaced by Christians. The work place was transformed in a matter of months. I got Wally a job on the team and everyone helped each other.

The home situation was in stark contrast to the one at work. I arrived back at the flat at about four in the morning and slept till nine, when I had to get up in order to be at the morning prayer meeting at ten. Reggie and Patsy were always in bed when I left, and when I returned the place was still in a mess. They didn't even bother to wash up the mugs. The strained atmosphere in the flat reminded me of prison just before trouble breaks out. I talked about the situation with Pastor Mike. He told me that I had no right to tell our 'guests' what to do, and suggested we drew up a cleaning rota. I felt OK about it for a few days, but then all the old resentment flooded back and tension within the flat mounted. Life at home steadily worsened, then one night I arrived back from work and discovered that Reggie and Patsy had gone. I was relieved but puzzled. They hadn't shown any signs of going, in fact quite the opposite. They'd appeared so determined to stay that I thought we'd never get rid of them.

The next morning, I asked Mel what had happened. He said that Reggie had accused him of looking at Patsy. He'd called Mel a nonce and Mel had told him that if he didn't like it he could go. It developed into quite an argument. Finally Reggie and Patsy packed their bags and left. I told Mel he should learn a lesson from this, and be more selective when it came to inviting people to stay. At last he seemed to see reason and the next two days passed peacefully. The peace was shattered the following evening when there was a knock at the door. Standing on the doorstep were Reggie and Patsy surrounded by their baggage. They said they'd come to apologize, but their intention was clear. They wanted to move back in. I stood firm and told them they'd really upset Mel, and it was best if we left things as they were. They saw that they weren't going to get anywhere with me so, reluctantly, they picked up their bags and went on their way.

Although it was quiet in the flat, Mel's seeming inability to tidy up or wash up annoyed me. When he brought a homeless old man back one night I became very upset. The old chap only stayed overnight, but I had visions of Reggie and Patsy turning up while I was out and Mel letting them back in. I thought about moving out of Mel's and getting a room on my own. It was nine months since I had left the bedsit but now I wished that I was back there.

Two weeks passed and I was still feeling the same. Another member of the church called round one evening. Mel was out, though we were due to go to home group at Pastor Mike's that night. I began to off-load all that was wrong with living with Mel onto our visitor, but half-way through my list of complaints Mel arrived, so I had to shut up. We had a cup of tea together, then the three of us walked up Ebury Bridge Road towards Victoria.

Suddenly I heard someone shout, 'Mick!' I looked round and saw Geoff Hunter and Kylie in a car. They signalled to me to come round the corner where they could pull into a car park. I left the others and caught up with Geoff and Kylie. Geoff told me he was doing well and invited me to jump into the car as he had some puff and, if I fancied it, we could drive somewhere and share a joint. I said it sounded tempting, but I was on my way to a meeting with a couple of people from church. Geoff said I'd only be missing one meeting, so did I want to come or not? I got in the car and we drove to Battersea Park.

We sat in the park and smoked a couple of joints, and I moaned for two hours solid about sharing a flat with Mel, and about other people in the church. Geoff couldn't let me have the bedsit because he'd rented it out to someone else, but he offered me the sofa at his and Kylie's flat until I could find somewhere better. I decided I could do with a break from Mel's and this seemed an ideal opportunity, so I asked Geoff when I could move in. 'Now, if you want to,' he replied. While Mel was still at home group, Geoff took me back to the flat. I packed up my belongings, posted the key through the door and left.

That night at Kylie's, we got well and truly stoned. I woke the following morning feeling bad about the complaints I'd made against the church, and some of the people in it. I wanted to tell Geoff that it had been a good night, but I thought I should go back to Mel's and the church. On the other hand, if I was honest with myself, I didn't want to be back at Mel's. Living there had become progressively worse and I had nowhere else to stay. As I wrestled with the dilemma of what to do next, Geoff and Kylie came through to the living room, and soon we were eating cornflakes and sharing a joint for breakfast. By midday we were stoned and getting into the cider and I pushed all thoughts of the church to the back of my mind. After an endless stream of joints and cider, we finished the night with a few Valium tablets, ready to repeat the pattern the next day and every day after that for a fortnight.

In all that time, I hadn't been to work and what money I had soon disappeared, so I thought I'd go back to selling *The Big Issue* to make some money. I started selling outside Chalk Farm tube station early in the morning, finishing at 10 am, by which time I would have made enough money to buy an eighth of an ounce of puff. I bought it from Geoff's supplier, then went back to Kylie's flat to have a smoke with her and Geoff. We spent the rest of each day in the West End, selling drugs that Kylie got on prescription.

Geoff and Kylie would walk round together looking for customers while I followed a little way behind. I had a telescopic cosh tucked into the back of my jeans in case there was any trouble, as selling drugs on the front line to junkies is a very risky business. You have to ensure that the junkie actually has the money to pay for the drugs. A junkie will do anything for a hit if he/she is clucking (starting to feel withdrawal symptoms from heroin). They might run off with the drugs or pull a knife and steal them from you. There is also the risk that the police will spot you. I was unlikely to be arrested if they got Geoff and Kylie because I kept some way away from them, but I knew I wasn't safe from the surveillance cameras.

Most afternoons I sold *The Big Issue* from a pitch outside a Safeway supermarket. The guy whose pitch it was finished at 3.30 pm, so I did a three-hour stint till 6.30 pm. Whatever money I took went straight on drink and drugs. I only thought about the church and the people there during the early hours of the morning, or when I was watching television. I was both shocked and surprised by how quickly my life had reverted to how it had been before I met Meg. I realized I was deliberately avoiding the area around Victoria in case I bumped into someone from the church. One morning I saw my suit hanging up in the wardrobe and I felt so ashamed. Pastor Mike had given me that suit and it was the best outfit I'd worn in years. It made me feel part of the church when I wore it to services, and I remembered how Mel and I had enjoyed getting suited and booted for Sunday morning service. Yet after all the help I'd been given, I'd just walked out without a word to anybody. Worst of all, I'd turned my back on God.

I decided to tell Geoff first thing next morning that I was leaving and going back to the church. Once Geoff was up and dressed I told him what I intended to do. He argued with me. There was no life after death, he insisted. The church had told me a load of rubbish. He'd saved me from hearing more of the same. As the discussion between us ebbed and flowed, Kylie kept rolling joints and passing them around. Soon we quietened down under the influence of the dope. Before I knew it, I was on my way to the West End with Kylie and Geoff to sell drugs. I forgot all about moving out of Kylie's flat.

The weeks flew by and the only change I made in my life was to start back at my old cleaning job. I did it to give Geoff and Kylie some privacy at night. The people I used to work with had left, and I wasn't sure whether I was pleased about this or not. On the one hand, I would have liked the comfort of having Christians around to pray with and for me, but on the other hand, without them, it wouldn't matter if I went to work half stoned.

I was careful to avoid meeting anyone from church, because I didn't want them to tell me what I already knew – that my lifestyle was wrong. Bit by bit I hardened my heart against all that I believed in. Weeks turned into months, and Kylie and Geoff's relationship went downhill. Geoff decided he needed some time away from Kylie and headed out of town for a couple of weeks. He asked me to make sure Kylie was OK, but within a few days Kylie brought another bloke back to the flat and was sleeping with him. She was ready to finish with Geoff when he'd only been away a week. I told this new bloke of hers that she already had a boyfriend and he was due back within forty-eight hours, so he should push off quickly. The bloke replied that it was up to Kylie to finish with him, and nothing to do with me. I warned him there'd be trouble, but he wasn't bothered. He should have been – Geoff was an aggressive fighter who'd done a fair bit of amateur boxing in his time.

Whenever I could get Kylie on her own, I tried to get her to sort out the mess she'd got herself into. She had to either get rid of the new bloke or tell Geoff to go. If she chose to ditch Geoff, then I felt I should look for somewhere else to stay. We talked and talked about it, gradually getting stoned and never reaching a definite decision. Then Geoff came back. Kylie didn't want to open the door to him and when she finally let him in his suspicions had already been aroused. He looked at me and asked if everything had been OK. 'Yeah, fine,' I replied. The moment passed and we settled down to smoke a few joints and chat.

During the next few weeks, Kylie and Geoff started rowing seriously. When I came back from work one morning Geoff wasn't around, and Kylie had a black eye. The bloke she'd slept with while Geoff was away had phoned up when she was out. Geoff had taken the call. When she came home they had a big row. Geoff hit her and stormed out. He was gone for two days. We tried to carry on as usual. I helped Kylie sell her drugs, and come the evening, we got out of our heads in an attempt to lessen our feelings of fear and trepidation. I knew I didn't stand a chance in a one-on-one fight with Geoff, but what really worried me was whether Geoff blamed me for what had happened. If so, he might come back and do some serious injury to Kylie and me. On the other hand, he might go after Kylie's new 'boyfriend', in which case I feared for the bloke's life. There was another possibility. We might never see Geoff again. The only answer for Kylie and me seemed to lie in heroin and puff and getting wrecked.

Four days later Geoff turned up. Over the next couple of days, to my relief, things seemed to settle down. I told Geoff I had lost my cleaning job and was selling *The Big Issue* again, so I'd be out most of the day but back about 6 pm. He didn't know that Kylie had begged me not to leave her alone with him during the night time. On my way home, I would phone up and find out if they wanted me to buy some puff and cider, and I often bought something for us to eat too. Then one day, out of the blue, trouble erupted.

Kylie was preparing the food I'd brought back, when Geoff started to have a go at me. He said I was to blame for what had happened between Kylie and the other bloke. I should have beaten him up and thrown him out. I explained to him that I had told the guy about him, and that it was up to Kylie to tell him to leave, not me. Geoff called Kylie in from the kitchen and asked if what I'd said was true. She hesitated for a moment, then said yes. Geoff began to get really angry. 'That's the trouble with you Christians,' he fumed, 'you're full of advice but do nothing to help.' He ordered me to go outside where he'd show me how I should have helped him. He was spoiling for a fight, but surprisingly, I felt quite calm. 'I class you as a good mate, Geoff,' I said, 'and I don't want to fight you.' He spat out his reply. 'I want to sort this out now.' I got to my feet. 'I'll go outside with you, Geoff, but I'm not going to fight you.'

There was a moment's silence. Geoff seemed unsure of himself, but then he moved towards the door and told me to come with him. As we walked to the entrance way that led to the car park, I kept thinking, 'This is stupid. Why am I going outside when I'm not going to fight him?' He stopped. I faced him and put my hands behind my back. He punched me in the head. The first punch cut open my forehead, the second knocked me to the ground. Geoff helped me up. His anger seemed spent and, as we walked back to the flat, he said he was sorry for hitting me and would understand if I didn't want to forgive him. I told him I'd forgiven him before he'd even hit me. The subject was dropped, and we made major inroads into our supply of drugs and booze.

The following afternoon after I'd finished selling *The Big Issue*, I phoned up as usual. Geoff answered. He said I'd messed his life up and he didn't want me at the flat anymore. Then he put the phone down on me. I bought some puff and cider, got drunk and stoned, and crashed out on a park bench for the night.

I woke up the next morning stiff, cold, depressed and uncertain of what to do. I went to a nearby caff, then back to the park. I felt lost. I couldn't go back to Geoff and Kylie, and the thought of returning to Mel's flat made me feel so guilty and ashamed that I knew I couldn't face anyone from the church. I had nowhere to go and no one to turn to. I went over what had happened at Kylie's and how I'd told Geoff he was already forgiven before he landed a punch. Would I be forgiven if I went back to the church?

One thing was certain, I wasn't going to waste a day hanging around in the park and I didn't want to sleep rough again. *The Big Issue* office had a department which helped people who needed accommodation. The office had moved to Farringdon, so I went straight there. After I'd explained my situation to Hannah, who was part of the housing team, she started ringing around on my behalf. Eventually she found a Salvation Army hostel that was willing to take me. She warned me that it would be a bit ropey because it was being closed down, but while I was there she'd try and find me something better.

I made my way to Bayswater and found the hostel. The major in charge took my details and said I could have a room, but it would be a temporary arrangement as the hostel was closing for renovation. He showed me to a double room which I could have to myself. As I looked round and saw the two wardrobes and chests of drawers, I realized that I had nothing to put in them. All I owned was at Kylie's flat and I didn't want to go back there, not even to pick up my clothes.

Over the next few days I sorted out my dole money and housing benefit and went out selling *The Big Issue*, returning to the hostel at tea time. The Salvation Army and *The Big Issue* office gave me some clothes and, with the money I was earning, I was able to buy some bits for myself. Every day I visited my supplier and every night I was out of my head on heroin, Valium or whatever drugs I'd managed to get. I'd smoke a joint in my room then take the drugs I'd bought. Once I felt them start to take effect I'd go and sit in Hyde Park with a few cans of cider. I wasn't alone. Some of the other blokes from the hostel went to the park for a few cans. Most of them were alcoholics, so it didn't take me long to find a drinking partner.

Sam was a drinker, but he kept himself clean and tidy. We soon became good friends. We stopped going to the park and instead stood outside Bayswater tube station drinking cider and having a good laugh. Sam wanted to know how I'd ended up in a hostel. I told him about prison and church and how I felt when I was filled with the Holy Spirit. Sam was quite interested until I got to the bit about the Holy Spirit. He decided I'd had too much to smoke! I resolved to keep religion out of the conversation, which was no problem when I was sober, but once I'd had a drink or two I'd go on at Sam about Jesus. He said as soon as I mentioned Jesus it was a sure sign that I was either drunk or stoned.

The need to go back to the church grew stronger and stronger, but I couldn't bring myself to do it. What would people think of me after all the help they'd given me? I decided to start selling *The Big Issue* at Victoria Coach Station again. If Wally, Mel or someone who knew me from the church came along, I would be able to gauge from their reaction whether they wanted to have anything to do with me or not. Day after day went by and I saw no one I knew. Then I fell out with Sam. It was about him registering a pitch in Victoria where he was going to sell *The Big Issue*. He lied to me about it, and it made me so angry I threatened to beat him up. That night he was nowhere to be seen. The following morning I felt bad about how I'd reacted. I knocked on his door so we could go down to breakfast together. There was no answer then, nor later that morning. He didn't show up at Victoria or back at the hostel or outside Bayswater tube station. Sam had gone for good.

I became more and more drunk every night. It was a wonder they let me into the hostel, as one of the rules is that you must be sober. A person who's drunk is likely to start trouble, or may choke to death on his vomit when he's asleep. Night after night, I lurched into the hostel hardly able to walk upright. I quite expected to be thrown out when the hostel closed, but I was given a form to fill in and promised an interview to sort out another hostel. Meanwhile Hannah said she might be able to get me into a house with four other people, where I could stay for two years.

One night, as I was drinking on my own outside Bayswater tube station, a woman approached and asked if she might have a swig of my cider. I gave her the can and we chatted. She was called Diana and was quite well dressed, but her face was hard and I could tell she was well used to a life of drink and drugs. I bought some more cans and went back with her to her bed and breakfast hotel, just a hundred yards down the road from my hostel. Diana was into heroin and was seven months pregnant. As we settled down in her room she asked if I used heroin. 'It has been known,' I replied and we were soon having a hit together and grouching out. I slept there that night. The next day I discovered that Diana was an expert shoplifter. When she found out how short of clothes I was she took me round the shops with her. Unfortunately the two of us were always followed by store detectives, so we went to charity shops instead, where it was easier to shoplift.

Diana and I became firm friends. She too used to go to church, though she'd left for different reasons from me. Now she was expecting a baby who would be born a heroin addict. I remembered a passage from the Bible that said if you cleaned up your life then turned away from God, you would open yourself up to demonic forces, and the demon you'd got rid of originally would return with seven others worse than himself. As I took stock of my situation, I thought this could well be true, and where did that leave me? It left me desperate for more heroin, so I could forget about God and the Bible and my situation. I wanted to be completely numb, to feel nothing.

Brad lived in the same bed and breakfast hotel as Diana. He too was into heroin and they would borrow a hit from each other when they were clucking or share it when they had plenty. One day Diana and I had done really well shoplifting and had got a good deal from our supplier, so she suggested we invite Brad in for a hit. I agreed. I liked Brad and soon we had the heroin on the spoon and in our arms. I took the same amount as usual, but the effect was very different. I passed out. The colour drained from my face and, according to Diana, I started to go blue. I had ODed on heroin and was at death's door. I didn't know anything about it until the next day when I regained consciousness, and she told me that I had Brad to thank for saving my life. He had sat me up, slapped my face and stopped me from slipping away. 'It's not Brad I ought to thank,' I thought to myself, 'but Jesus.'

Twelve

Under Pressure

I was sitting on a bench in Hyde Park less than forty-eight hours after ODing. I had a can of cider in my hand and I was thinking about how to get right with God again. It occurred to me that I could save myself from any embarrassment by going to a different church. Then I saw someone walking towards me, and I wished the ground would open and swallow me up. It was Andy, who used to play bass guitar with the worship team at church. He was a really nice guy and, as soon as he saw me, he stopped for a chat. He made light of the can I was holding and peered behind the bench, jokingly asking where I'd stashed the rest of the booze. Before we went our separate ways, he said, 'You can't tell me you're ashamed to go back to church. I saw how on fire you were for God,' and I admitted to him that I knew I should go back.

That night, Diana told me that she had seen her care worker and was going to be offered a place in Brighton, where she and her baby would be looked after until the baby was old enough to be taken into care. Diana knew that her drug addiction meant she wouldn't be able to bring up her child herself. She wanted to go to Brighton, and I said I thought it would be better for her than being stuck in one room in a hotel. She said she'd be going within the next two weeks and asked me to visit her when she got there.

I woke the next day determined to go back to the church. I walked across Hyde Park to Victoria and made it to the building which housed the church office just in time for the 10 o'clock morning prayer meeting. I was about to go in, when I thought I just need one can to calm my nerves. I spent all that day in Battersea Park getting totally wrecked. I went back to the hostel that night instead of Diana's, and attempted to sleep off the effects of too much cider. The following day I discovered that I had no money left. I couldn't buy any copies of *The Big Issue* – I was skint. I ate breakfast and decided again to make it to the church office. With no money for a bus, I walked and was only part way there when it began to rain heavily. I thought about turning back and going round to Diana's for the day, but suddenly I felt a surge of steely determination rise up inside me and I kept going, walking from tree to tree as the thunder rolled and lightning split open the sky. By the time I reached the other side of the park the rain had eased up. To my surprise I'd managed to keep relatively dry.

I walked into the church office. People turned round as I came into the room. Their faces were a picture. Sophie started jumping up and down with delight, saying, 'This is an answer to prayer!' Pastor Mike told me that the church members had been praying and fasting that week for people to return, as I wasn't the only one to have been tempted away. Later that day, I went back to the pastor's home and told him what had happened and why I thought it had happened.

Pastor Mike prayed with me and talked to me for a long time that night. He put my mind at rest over my problems sharing with Mel. He said I didn't have to live at Mel's. If I was happy in the hostel, then I should stay there until I felt I should move on. Then he told me something that really encouraged and excited me. He said I should look to go on with God, because God had things for me to do and he would enable me to do them. If at that point he had said, 'Mick, in two years time, you will be writing a book, having a video made of your life, helping take an Alpha course in prison, sharing your story with prisoners in Blundestone, running a book stall in church, preaching on the streets, giving your testimony in meetings and spending time with your parents,' I would probably have walked out thinking, 'You don't know what you're talking about.'

The pastor warned me that if we don't go forward with God, we usually slip back. He reminded me of the need for real repentance, and that I should forgive anyone against whom I held a grudge. I put this into practice the next day when I saw Mel. Within a couple of hours we were out on the streets together talking to people about the love of Jesus. I explained to Mel that I was going to stay in the Salvation Army hostel, but would get together with him regularly. He was pleased as Wally wasn't around much, and he would be glad of my company.

That same week, the Salvation Army told me I had a place in a new hostel which just happened to be in Victoria. I was so excited as I knew this was from God. I was making a new start, and whereas before I had had little to do with the other residents, now I sat with them at meal times and talked about my faith. People reacted in different ways, but it often led to some interesting conversations.

The church was only ten minutes walk away, and I was soon involved in all sorts of activities, from doing mailouts to setting up the sound equipment for services, as well as giving out tracts on the streets. The staff at the hostel noticed the change in me and I explained how I'd accepted Jesus as my personal Saviour, but had turned back to my old ways for a few months before returning to the church I was with before.

The hostel was brand new with single rooms for residents, a TV room on each floor and a communal canteen area where you were provided with breakfast and dinner. The major told us that the Queen was going to open the hostel officially on 12 December 1996. Those who didn't want to be filmed were asked to sign a form. I was happy to be filmed, and would have liked to have been one of the residents chosen to speak to the Queen, but a bloke called Luke was given this honour and had his moment of fame. Luke was an old punk rocker with 'Punk is not Dead' tattooed across his forehead, so I consoled myself with the thought that good looks were not one of the criteria for being selected!

Christmas came. The hostel was decorated and games and quizzes were organized. For me and many other residents, Christmas and the New Year brought back unhappy memories. I thought of the time I was living in Devon and rang my family to say I was coming home for Christmas. My parents told me to come in the New Year instead. My brother James said he was spending Christmas at Timothy's. I had decided none of my family wanted to see me and I took the presents I'd bought them back to the shops.

Then there were other Christmases when I was banged up and didn't even bother to phone my parents, convinced I'd get a cool reaction if I did. I cast my mind back to Christmas 1995. I was living in Mel's flat then and I'd written to my parents telling them that I'd changed my ways, but there was no reply to my letter. I wondered if they had ever received it. It had led to one of my bad days when I would get drunk and usually do something stupid. On that particular occasion I'd walked down the King's Road full of cider and passed a stall selling Christmas trees. Without thinking, I picked up a tree and continued towards Victoria, arriving at Mel's flat without anyone challenging me. The following morning I woke up feeling really bad about what I'd done, so I phoned Pastor Mike. He came round and told me I could either go and pay for the tree or take it back. I explained that I hadn't the money to pay for it and if I took it back it would lose so many of its needles on the way that the stall holder probably wouldn't accept it anyway. In the end I went back to the stall, admitted to the owner that I'd stolen one of his trees and asked him if he could come and pick it up! The stall holder was remarkably calm about it and came round later in a van to collect his property.

I was determined not to make a mistake like that again this Christmas. I had a good time with Wally and Mel, and received a card from Wally with a picture on it of a bear carrying a Christmas tree up the road. My antics of Christmas 1995 had not been forgotten! The Salvation Army gave me a card too, and a china mug and some sweets. I was touched that there were people who cared about me. I saw in the New Year at the church office, where we enjoyed the music of our guest singer, Dizzy K.

At the start of 1997 I was back out selling *The Big Issue* on a registered pitch outside Fortnum and Masons, Piccadilly. There were two other *Big Issue* sellers, Neil and Carl, in the vicinity. We got on well together and helped each other out. As for accommodation – I was hoping to get one of the flats behind the hostel. If my application was successful, I'd have my own room and share a kitchen and bathroom with four others. The rent was lower than the hostel because residents in the flats had to cook for themselves.

In my spare time, I continued to be actively involved with doing mailouts and going out preaching on the streets. Sometimes I became annoyed when people who had promised to help didn't turn up, and I made it a principle that if I was unable to attend a meeting or help when I was expected to, I would phone up beforehand. The importance of everyone doing their bit became extra clear when Pastor Kunle announced one Sunday that we were moving into

City Temple that coming week. He had arranged a line-up of well-known preachers and singers which would keep us busy for at least six months. Our small church, numbering fifty members, was going to be responsible for events normally organized by churches which had hundreds of members to call on. We drew up a twenty-four-hour prayer rota so that people would be praying around the clock, but we had no idea of the workload we would be facing.

Phone calls started coming in from around the globe. There were hotel bookings to be made, letters to send, endless inquiries to deal with. Meanwhile the person who rented the church office to us asked if we could confine ourselves to a smaller space. We did so, only for the landlord to come back after a few weeks and suggest we split our new office space into two offices, of which we could have the larger one. Again we agreed. I was spending more and more time working in the office, and filling in for people who were on the prayer rota but didn't honour their commitment for one reason or another. What really got to me, though, was the number of helpers who complained that things weren't being done in the way they thought best. As far as I could see, those who moaned most were the least likely to volunteer to do anything extra.

Despite such problems, the first event, the African Children's Choir, went extremely well. The place was packed every night. Pastor Kunle and Mel had given up their flats to accommodate the choir and their helpers. We bought dozens of sleeping bags and underlays, but when we discovered there were forty children, we had to send some of them to stay in the homes of church members. These children are the best in the world. Most of them have lost one or both parents, have seen people killed and experienced famine. Yet they are full of love and joy. I stayed with Mel and ten of the boys from the choir in Pastor Kunle's flat, and every morning they would sing for us as we prepared their breakfast. In the evenings we had our own private concert and I felt privileged to spend a week in the company of these children. After they left for their next tour we were bombarded with requests for tapes of their singing and news of our next event.

As the workload increased, so the pressure and tension built up. Some people seemed intent on undermining others, some wanted to take control, others were convinced that only they knew the right way to do the various tasks we faced. It was at times like this that I found my experience of prison discipline a great help. I was prepared to do whatever was asked of me without complaining or arguing. Sometimes I didn't know why I was doing a certain job, but as long as I was serving God that was more than enough for me.

I seemed to be the only one who had noticed the atmosphere of ever-increasing stress and strain amongst the church members. I suppose my years in prison made me particularly sensitive to the mood of a group of people, and I could certainly sense trouble afoot.

There was more grief from our landlord. Although we now had a smaller office, he was still not satisfied and wrote to Pastor Mike giving him notice to quit. Peter Youngren, who runs a large

Bible school in Canada and is also well known for his healing ministry, was the focus of our next event and he was already on his way to the UK. It was vital that we had an office which was manned around the clock, not just for this event but for the other crusades which were happening in the following weeks. Although the pressure was intense and never seemed to lift, I enjoyed it. It was exciting and it re-focused my thoughts. Never again would I assume that people who went to church were passive and boring.

Peter Youngren arrived and was soon heavily involved in daytime seminars and evening meetings. The meetings were videotaped and, as we held the copyright, we were able to sell copies. This added to our workload and there was still the worry over the office. Pastor Mike explained to me that he only had a verbal agreement with the landlord who, two years ago, had been very keen to rent office space to the church, since at that time it was difficult to find lessees. The pastor had asked for a contract because he wanted the office on a permanent basis, but the landlord had given his word and implied that that was sufficient.

I had a set of keys to the office and went there at five every morning. The prayer rota was continuing, although some hours weren't covered, as people either didn't keep up their commitment or decided they'd rather pray at home. One or two had even left to join another church. Pastor Kunle was often there when I arrived and at 6 am another church member, Bridgett, came to pray before she went to work.

One Sunday Pastor Mike went to the office, only to find it full of furniture which had been dumped there from another office. Our office had been unmanned for most of the day. I helped the pastor move the furniture and we decided that someone should be in the office from early the next morning. I volunteered, and I hadn't been there long before the landlord's wife arrived and told me to leave. I replied that I was not in charge. She would have to see Pastor Mike when he came at 10 am. The woman kept on at me, so in the end, I ignored her and went on praying. At this point she threatened to call the police. I looked her straight in the eyes. 'You can call whoever you like,' I told her levelly, 'but I am praying and I'll go on praying until 10 o'clock.' Her face red with anger, the woman stormed off to phone the police. I moved the generator we used for powering equipment on the streets behind the door and continued to pray.

The door was tried several times, and then a voice outside announced that he was a policeman and he wanted to speak to me. I moved the generator and opened the door. An officer held out a letter to me. He asked if I'd received a copy. I pointed out that it was addressed to Pastor M. Burgess who would be at the office at 10 o'clock. 'Now, if you don't mind,' I said to the police, 'I'm praying.' 'The lady wants you to leave,' one of them responded. I refused to leave. The church was renting the office. I prayed there every morning and I wasn't going to make an exception that day or any other. The police tried a harder line. They accused me of trespass and of breaking and entering. I dangled the keys in front of them – they were for the office and the downstairs door which led out on to the street. The police backtracked and asked me to leave more politely. They said the pastor could sort it out later. I asked them why they didn't leave. I could go on praying and the woman could talk to the pastor when he arrived.

The police tried a different tack. Why did I need to pray in that particular place? I explained that it was an office and if the phone rang it needed to be answered. One of them decided to try and needle me. 'You're not really a Christian, are you?' he said. 'Yes I am,' I replied. If I was a Christian, he said, I wouldn't be making such a fuss about leaving the office. I described to him the way in which the landlord had reduced our space until we had only a corner of a room to work from, and how he had promised we would not be forced to leave, but the police had heard enough. They wanted me out and they gave me a choice. I could either leave of my own free will or they would arrest me. 'They arrested Jesus and he was innocent,' I said, 'so you'll have to arrest me too.' I was arrested for trespassing, handcuffed and led out of the building. Outside they told me they didn't really want to arrest me, and asked what I would do if they were to release me there on the street. I said I'd go back into the office and carry on praying. 'I've got the keys, remember,' I reminded them. In that case, they told me, they'd have to take me to the police station. As they put me in the police car, Sophie came down the road. I quickly told her what was happening, and she went straight away to fetch Pastor Mike.

At the police station I went through the normal booking-in procedure, then they locked me in a cell. I was allowed to keep my Bible and after reading for a while I started singing hymns. The duty sergeant kept checking up on me, as if he thought I was a suicide risk. Meanwhile Pastor Mike had arrived and was telling the police about the office situation. He kept insisting that an officer reported back to him regularly as to my wellbeing. It took a few hours, but finally the police dropped the charges against me and released me, asking for no more than my word that I would not go back to the office. Pastor Mike went there, only to find that it had been emptied of all our equipment, including the church computer which had been unplugged and dumped at the bottom of the stairs by the main entrance. Everything had to be taken to Pastor Mike's or Pastor Kunle's for storage before it was lost or stolen. Pastor Kunle said we could use his spare room as an office and a place where people could continue to pray around the clock. It meant he had church members coming and going at all hours of the day and night.

Our next event centred around a preacher from America who wasn't as well-known as others we had booked. We had, however, spent a lot of time and effort advertising his seminars including flyers, mailouts and announcements on Premier Radio. When only a couple of dozen people turned up at the City Temple on the first night, we were surprised and disappointed, and I began to think that those who'd moaned and groaned about the work involved and the organization might have a point. Then it occurred to me that it was OK while I was doing all the running around and helping out on a voluntary basis, but what if I wanted paying for the hours I put in? One of the helpers, Liza, had given up because it took up too much of her time, leaving me, Pastor Mike and Pamela to do the office work. As Pamela had a full-time job she could only lend a hand after 6 pm, so, as the next event featuring Barry Smith got nearer, the pressure was really on. I had no time to sell *The Big Issue*, but when I mentioned this to Pastor Kunle he promised I would be paid. This took a weight off my mind, and I was further encouraged by comments from the staff at the hostel about how much I'd changed, but the workload went on growing.

By the time Barry Smith flew in from New Zealand, it seemed that no one was prepared to assist with the ushering or taking up the offering, let alone setting up the sound equipment. I had the job of asking people to help, and almost everyone came up with an excuse. Bridgett and I, who were totally inexperienced, had to set up the sound system working from the instruction manual. During the meeting I was involved with taking the offering, and afterwards I sat at the back of the hall selling videos, audio tapes and CDs. Barry Smith had his own agents in the foyer, also selling his books and videos. There were meetings every night, five nights in a row, and the place was packed.

What really stressed me out, though, was when things were changed at the last minute and nobody told me why. It was at the close of the third night of the crusade when Pastor Kunle came over to me and told me not to sell the new set of Barry Smith videos but to pack them away. When I asked why, he just repeated his request and moved off. I reckoned Barry Smith's agents wanted all the business. This annoyed me and once I got annoyed everyone knew about it. When someone came over to me and tried to calm me down, saying, 'Look, we're all just trying to serve God,' I snapped. 'I can serve God in any church,' I replied and walked out. I headed down the road towards Farringdon tube station, still fuming.

Someone put a restraining hand on my arm. It was Pamela. She'd run after me and caught me just before I reached the station. She told me how much they all appreciated the work I was doing, and how encouraged they were by the change in me. Pamela said no one wanted to see me slip back into my old way of life and she begged me to come back to the meeting and stay, until they packed up for the evening. I refused. I'd had enough for that day and I wanted to go home and think about whether or not I'd attend the next meeting. What Pamela said to me that night didn't touch me as much as the fact that she'd cared enough to run after me, but despite that I didn't ring Pastor Mike or go to the morning prayer meeting. Instead I walked across Hyde Park and did some window shopping.

By the evening I was feeling much better, and I went to the Barry Smith meeting. Pastor Mike gave me a warm welcome and told me if I wanted to help that was fine, but if I didn't that was OK too. I said I'd come to help and explained that I'd got angry the previous evening because Barry Smith's agents had stopped me selling his videos. The Pastor smiled wryly. I'd been asked to remove the videos from sale, he said, only because that particular batch were faulty. I felt a right idiot. I half mumbled 'sorry' and beat a hasty retreat. All evening I kept thinking I must go and apologize to Pastor Kunle, but I couldn't do it. It wasn't my fault, I told myself, pushing to the back of my mind the way I'd flown off the handle and stormed out. I don't think I ever offered an apology to Pastor Kunle, but I never walked out of another meeting, although the crusades which we organized over the next three months brought with them similar pressures and problems.

By the time it was all over we were only left with between ten and fifteen church members. Instead of gaining numbers we had lost people. Pastor Kunle reminded us of a sermon he'd preached before the events started. He'd warned us then that we were going to go through a tough time together. You will be shaken, he told us, but those of you who stick with it will be used by God as pillars of his church. As the weeks went by, new people joined us, including a family from Holland, who believed God wanted them to be in London. David and Angelique sold their house and, with their children, came to live in England. They joined the Holy Nation Church and lived off the proceeds of their house sale. They have been a great support to me in the two and a half years they have spent in this country. Although our church was small, I knew it was where God wanted me to be and that its members were committed people who longed to be used by God.

As I have discovered, and shared in this book, being a Christian is not easy, but following Jesus gives you a joy in your life that surpasses all understanding.

God doesn't care who you are or what you've done. He can take your life and turn it around if you let him. He can humble the proud or take the filthiest beggar from the street and cause him to be like a shining diamond for Jesus. As for me – today I can tell people that I am a new creation, and I know that anyone who really wants to can come into God's kingdom and be changed from glory into glory.

A New Creation

The transformation in Mick's life since he became a Christian has been truly remarkable. During his time in Satan's Breed, and throughout his life of crime, Mick did have times when he enjoyed himself, but such times were fleeting and he was always looking for something new and exciting to give some meaning to his life. Mick appeared to be a fun-loving, couldn't-care-less sort of bloke but, in reality, he was desperately unhappy. He was miserable, unfulfilled, lonely, insecure and angry.

Before his conversion, Mick's habitual response to anything or anybody was sarcastic, critical and cold. But now his life has taken on a whole new dimension. He is warm, caring and full of joy. Of course he faces problems and difficult situations, but he is no longer alone. He knows that Jesus is with him and will help him through the tough times and that every trial and storm in his life is used by God to work everything out for good.

After twenty-six years of living in prisons, hostels, with friends and on the streets, Mick has, at last, got a home of his own. The Salvation Army recently allocated him a flat in Hackney. Mick prayed hard about this big change in his life. He thought he might be placed in a high-rise block on a run-down estate where drugs and crime were rife. Mick needn't have worried. He was given a flat in a brand-new block of just four flats. It is secure, clean and big enough to accommodate the occasional guest and Mick is always the first to offer his sofa to someone for a few nights until they find a hostel that will take them.

Mick is still in and out of prison – but now it's voluntary! He's very much involved in Wandsworth and Brixton prisons, running an Alpha course in one and evening meetings in the other. Mick can empathize with the prisoners and when they hear his testimony they realize, perhaps for the first time in their lives, that the gospel message is for them as well as the rest of us on the outside. Through Chaplaincy groups and Bible studies, Mick builds friendships with inmates and many of them write to him. He replies with letters of encouragement and sends them cassettes of Christian music and teaching. Mick often attends court cases with remand prisoners or those on appeal, and visits inmates who have no one coming to see them. Once a week, he organizes a prayer meeting for all the prisoners with whom he is in contact.

For all the expenses he incurs in this ministry to prisoners, Mick supports himself financially. He has found it virtually impossible to find a job because of his extensive criminal record, so he continues to earn a living by selling *The Big Issue*. Mick also preaches the gospel on the streets of central London. He shares with passers-by how Jesus has revolutionized his life, prays with anyone who requests prayer and hands out leaflets explaining the way to salvation.

Mick is very involved in the Holy Nations Church. He faithfully attends the services, prayer meetings, home groups and other activities and he's always willing to serve and help out in whatever way he can. This man, who used to be so stubborn, rebellious and defiant, who refused to take orders from anyone, is the first to volunteer for any task, however mundane. Mick's new life has a focus. With Jesus at the core of what he is and does, he looks outwards to the needs of others instead of inwards. Now, at last, he knows true fulfilment.

The loneliness which dogged Mick from childhood has melted away. He always believed he was academically inferior to his siblings and, because he messed around at school, he usually came bottom of the class. He felt that he didn't fit in and this feeling was accentuated when he turned to a life of crime. Even in the bike gangs and among crowds of friends, he never felt totally accepted for who he was. He convinced the people he went round with that he was one of them, but deep inside he was desperately alone. Most of that loneliness was banished when Jesus Christ fully accepted Mick with wide open arms and any such feelings that remained were dissolved by the love and warmth he has received within the church. Mick is popular. He has made many friends and proved himself to be a really loyal guy who never lets you down and is always there for you when you need him.

After he became a Christian, Mick really wanted a true and lasting reconciliation with his family, particularly with his parents. Two years ago he travelled to Basingstoke to visit them. He set off with great anxiety and trepidation, not knowing if they were still alive, and if they were, how they would react when they saw him. When he arrived on their doorstep, Mick didn't realize that it was the day of his Mum and Dad's Golden Wedding anniversary! Despite all that had happened, they welcomed him home. Mick's Dad said his return was the best anniversary present he could have received. Mick visits his parents from time to time, prays for them constantly and, with God's help and guidance, he is slowly restoring the broken relationships in his family. He hopes that, one day, by God's grace, he will be fully reconciled to all the members of his family.

Mick is no longer 'Mr Angry'! He built up a reputation as a hard man because he wanted an identity and a sense of security. He used to lose his temper easily, storm off, resort to violence and take revenge on anyone he thought had wronged him. Jesus has changed all that. Now Mick has an inner peace, he's no longer scared or insecure. When he shares the gospel on the streets, he lays himself open to abuse. He has been punched in the head, had bottles, beer and even dog food thrown at him and has been arrested for street preaching. On every occasion, he has remained steadfast to Jesus and has turned the other cheek.

What does the future hold? A documentary of Mick's life, made by the Inspiration Network Christian TV Channel in 2000, is due to be broadcast at the same time as this book is published. As news of

Mick's story has spread, he has started to receive invitations to share his testimony and it is likely that the number of Mick's speaking engagements will increase. Mick himself has a deep longing to go into more prisons and travel to many nations so that he can share his wonderful story of how Jesus Christ has changed his life.

Pastor Mike.

If you want to contact Mick Whitburn, you can do so by writing to him:

c/o Holy Nations Church, PO Box 4215, Victoria, LONDON, SW1E 5XH, United Kingdom
or e-mail: Info@holynationchurch.org

Glossary

Prison slang

Bang up	time to go to your cell
Banged up	locked in a cell
Boss	prison officer
Bottled	drugs hidden up back passage
Burn	tobacco
Chokey	solitary confinement
Civvies	your own clothing
Civvy	cigarette brand name
Con	prisoner
Creased	drugs held between the buttocks
Dear John	letter from partner finishing relationship
Diesel	cup of tea
Do your bird	tell someone to do their sentence
Dog ends	cigarette ends
Doing a deal	buying or selling drugs
Doing bird	serving a prison sentence

Doing time	serving a prison sentence
Dry bath	strip search
E man	prisoner who escaped or attempted to escape
Fag butts	cigarette ends
43 Case	sex offender
Fraggle	prisoner with learning difficulties
Fraggle rock	special landing for prisoners with learning difficulties
Framed	to put something illegal in someone's cell and tell on them
Get done	to lose a fight
Ghosted	moved from one prison to another without warning
God squad	church-goers
Gov	prison officer
Holding	in possession of drugs
Hooch	alcohol made in prison
In nick	serving a prison sentence
In patches	prisoner who escaped or attempted to escape
Jam roll	parole
Kit	prison clothing
Knock back	refused parole
Lifer	a long prison sentence
Nonce	sex offender
On 43	prisoner on protection
On my pot	a short prison sentence
Own gear	Your own clothing
Pad	cell

Parcel	in possession of drugs
Peter	cell
Pit	bed
Planted	to put something illegal in someone's cell and tell on them
Rip off	to sell someone a short deal or fake drugs or to plant something on someone
Red band	trusted prisoner
Rizla	cigarette papers
Roll-up	tobacco
Roll-up	hand rolled cigarette
Rolly	hand rolled cigarette
Row	fight, argument
Rule 43	prisoner on protection
Screw	prison officer
Shipped out	moving from one prison to another without warning
Shxx and a shave	a short prison sentence
Skins	cigarette papers
Slop out	get water and empty chamber pot
Snout	tobacco
Spin	cell search
Stitch up	to sell someone a short deal or fake drugs or to plant something on someone
Stitched up	to put something illegal in someone's cell and tell on them

Stretch	a long prison sentence
Stripe up	cut someone with razor or knife
Sweat box	van that transports prisoners to and from prison
Swooping	picking up cigarette ends
Swoops	cigarette ends
Tailor-made	cigarette brand name
The block	solitary confinement
Tool	weapon
Tooled up	carrying a weapon
Topped	committed suicide
Two's/two's up	to share a cigarette
Wheeling and dealing	looking for people to sell to

Drugs

Acid	*see* LSD
Amps	small measure of drug for a hypodermic dose
Banging up	injecting
Bong	pipe for smoking cannabis
Cannabis	narcotic drug
Chalice	pipe for smoking cannabis
Chase the dragon	smoking heroin
Chasing	smoking heroin
Chillum	pipe for smoking cannabis
Come up	period between first effects of a drug and the full effects

Come down	period between full effects of a drug and normality
Cut	when a powder drug such as cocaine is mixed e.g. with glucose to make it stretch further
Dope	cannabis or heroin
Fix	injecting
Gear	heroin
Grass	buds and sometimes leaves of cannabis plant
Grouching out	feeling the effects of heroin
Hash	solid cannabis
Hit	injecting
Joint	cigarette containing marijuana
Lebanese (leb)	form of hash
LSD	hallucinogenic drug
Marijuana	dried hemp leaves smoked as an intoxicant
Moody	drugs which are fake or not up to standard
Papers	*see* Rizla
Physeptone	Methadone in tablet form
Puff	cannabis
Reffa	rolling a joint
Rizla	cigarette papers
Rocky	form of cannabis
Score	purchase the drug required
Script	prescription
Sensimillia	*see* Marijuana

Skin up	to make a joint to smoke
Skinning up	rolling a joint
Skins	cigarette papers
Smack	heroin
Speed	amphetamine
Stoned	effect of smoking dope
Tab	small amount of LSD
Trip	mind-altering hallucinating effect of LSD
Two skinner joint	two cigarette papers stuck together to make a larger joint
Weed	cannabis
Whack up	injecting
Works	syringes, needles for drug taking

Other

Bang to rights	caught in the act
Bluey	£5
Brassic	to have no money
Chill out	relax
Cockle	£10
Copper	police officer
Dosh	money
Firm	organized criminals
Grand	£1000
Grassed up	to inform
Ham and egg	beg
Hot bricks	goods that sell well
Jam sandwich	police car

Long one	£100
Moody	counterfeit
Muck	cement
Mummers	women
Mumble	to talk someone out of their money or goods
Nifty	£50
Oily rag	fag
Old Bill	police officer
On top	to be caught or about to be caught
Pear-shaped	for things to go wrong
Pig	police officer
Plunder	broken or damaged goods
Put on top	to inform
Rabbit	to talk
Red handed	caught in the act
Right on top	caught in the act
Rip off	steal
Road rash	heavy grazing
Score	£20
Screwing	to look at someone for a long time
Skid lid	motorcycle helmet
Skint	to have no money
Skipping	sleeping rough
Suited and booted	dressed up
Turn over	to burgle
24/7	to do something all the time
Up front	payment in advance
Wedged up	in possession of a lot of money

SERVING AS SENDERS

Neal Pirolo

ISBN 1-85078-199-0

"This key book makes the point that mobilizers – the senders – are as crucial to the cause of missions as frontline missionaries. It is a book just crammed with solid, exciting insights on the most hurting link in today's mission movement."

Ralph Winter
U.S. Centre for World Mission

"Unless the Church and God's people respond to this book's message, the work of reaching the unreached is going to be greatly hindered. Every committed sender needs to get involved in distributing this book."

George Verwer
Operation Mobilisation

Neal Pirolo is the founding Director of Emmaus Road International, San Diego, California, mobilizing churches, training cross-cultural teams, and networking fellowships with national ministries around the world.

OM
publishing

SERVING GOD TODAY

Martin & Elizabeth Goldsmith

ISBN 1-85078-364-0

Missionaries, prolific writers, college lecturers, internationally renowned conference speakers ... the resume continues! Martin and Elizabeth Goldsmith bring together a wealth of insights from their experience in Christian service around the globe in this marvellous collection of three of their popular titles.

Your Guide to Guidance
Choosing a job? Considering marriage? Facing a major family decision?
This book is packed with sensible and biblical advice that makes sense of the different ways God guides today, whatever your situation.

Kingdom Life: Signs, Justice or Holiness
Jesus taught His followers to pray 'Your kingdom come' – but on another occasion He said, 'The kingdom of God is within you.' So what did He mean by 'the kingdom'? Martin Goldsmith offers a challenging overview of this popular subject among evangelical Christians.

Going Places: Preparing for Christian Service
Does the thought that God might one day call you to work for him 'full-time' linger in the back of your mind? Maybe it will be at home or abroad, short-term or long-term, in the church, with students or some other kind of work – who knows? This is a book for those who want to be 'going places' for God.

OM
publishing

OPERATION WORLD

PRAY FOR THE WORLD

Patrick Johnstone

ISBN 1-85078-120-6

The definitive guide to praying effectively and specifically for every country of the world, formatted for daily use, or to dip into when praying for missionaries or around current events. Using this book is an excellent way to involve yourself in global mission.

STOP, CHECK, GO

Ditch Townsend

ISBN 1-85078-364-0

Anyone planning on going overseas on a short-term missions trip should soak up the contents of this invaluable book. Helping them to prepare practically, personally and spiritually, this superb book will ensure that the benefits of the experience are greatly increased to all concerned.

OUT OF THE COMFORT ZONE

George Verwer

ISBN 1–85078–353–5

Reading this book could seriously change your attitude! George Verwer has managed to write a book that is humble and hard-hitting at the same time. He doesn't pull any punches in his heart's cry for a 'grace-awakened' approach to mission, and wants to cut through superficial 'spirituality' that may be lurking inside you. George Verwer is known throughout the world as a motivator and mobiliser. *Out of the Comfort Zone* should only be read by those who are willing to accept God's grace, catch His vision and respond with action in the world of mission.

DISTINCTIVES

Vaughan Roberts

ISBN 1–85078–331–4

In a fresh and readable style, the author of *Turning Points*, Vaughan Roberts issues a challenging call to Christians to live out their faith. We should be different from the world around us — Christian distinctives should set us apart in how we live, think, act and speak. Targeting difficult and crucial areas such as our attitude to money and possessions, sexuality, contentment, relativism and service, this is holiness in the tradition of J.C. Ryle for the contemporary generation.

- Will you take up the challenge?
- Will you dare to be different?

Vaughan Roberts is rector of St Ebbe's Church, Oxford. He is a popular conference speaker and University Christian Union speaker.

THE GEORGE VERWER COLLECTION

ISBN 1-85078-296-2

George Verwer has inspired and encouraged thousands in their Christian discipleship. Now three of his best-loved books, *The Revolution of Love*, *No Turning Back*, and *Hunger For Reality* are brought together in this three in-one collection. The trilogy points us to love as the central theme of Christian life, calls us to effective service and revolutionizes our lives so that they are consistent and productive.

"Immensely readable and full of the practical aspects of spiritual principles."

Evangelicalism Today

"A wealth of good material."

Martin Goldsmith,
Church of England Newspaper

Over 100,000 copies sold.

George Verwer is the founder and International Director of Operation Mobilisation. He has an international preaching ministry based in Britain.

OM
publishing